WIKI

Grow Your Own for Fun and Profit

Alan J. Porter

WIKI
Grow Your Own for Fun and Profit
Copyright © 2010 Alan J. Porter

Graphics Credits

Cover Design:	Patrick Davison
Drawings:	Douglas Potter

Disclaimer

Trademarks

XML Press
Fort Collins, Colorado 80528
http://xmlpress.net

First Edition
ISBN: 978-0-9822191-2-6

Table of Contents

Foreword

I'm no Lone Ranger. But, I am The Content Wrangler. As a content strategist, I help organizations create, manage, and deliver the information they use to run their businesses, something most organizations are ill-prepared to do, at least not efficiently or effectively. Don't get me wrong, not every firm misses the mark. Some organizations do it right. But, chances are, your organization doesn't.

Don't be offended. That's not meant as an insult. Wrangling content is tricky proposition for most. It's a discipline, informed by years of information engineering research, made possible by an increasingly powerful array of software tools and guided by business decisions based on science and mathematics.

Most organizations have yet to master the art of content wrangling, let alone see the value in streamlining their content life cycle. But, it doesn't have to be this way. By taking time to examine how you do things today, you can find ways to improve the way you create, manage, and deliver information, too.

The First Step is Admitting You Have a Problem: You are Addicted to Software

The first step, as 12 step programs have touted for decades, is to admit you have a problem. Most organizations go about tackling content challenges by starting from the wrong vantage point. They don't start with the problem, they start by jumping toward what they believe is the solution – software. It's only natural. We've been programmed to think that software solves problems, when in reality, software introduces as many problems as it helps us to solve ... especially, when you select the wrong software tool for the job.

Avoiding the tool trap is easy. The first step is to admit you are addicted to software and that your addiction, like all addictions, can cause you to make decisions that may have very negative consequences. Don't allow yourself to start talking about software tools until you understand what your real challenges are. What problems are you trying to solve? Why are they problems? What do those problems cost your organization? And, what are you willing to do to make those problems go away?

Once you've identified what you think your problems are and what you're willing to do to solve them, it's time to start looking at the way that you do things today – your content life cycle. At a high level you are going to examine how you create, manage and deliver content.

More specifically, you will look for the things that slow you down and that impede your productivity. Are the manual tasks you perform today necessary or could they be automated? What roles and responsibilities will be different if you change the way you do things? What training will be required? How will these changes impact others who need access to your content? What people, processes, and systems rely on your content?

By understanding how you work today, you'll be able to build a model for how you would like to work tomorrow. And, once you know what your problems are, what you are willing to do to solve them, what your perfect solution looks like, and what changes will need to take place, you're ready to start talking about software tools.

The Wonderful World of Wikis

Wikis are one of the most powerful content production tools to be introduced in the Internet age. They can be configured to help you tackle all sorts of content challenges – managing simple authoring projects, implementing complex content collaboration projects, building customer support portals, and running large scale online communities. The possibilities are endless and limited only by your imagination and your willingness to think differently.

Use this book as a starting point for understanding wikis – what they are, how they work, and how others are using them to solve all sorts of content challenges. Wiki-master Alan Porter has provided you with everything you'll need to know to determine if a wiki might help you solve your content problems and, perhaps more importantly, whether a wiki will be a good fit for your organization.

Scott Abel, *The Content Wrangler*
August 28, 2010,
Palm Springs, CA

Preface

A wiki is more than just software for enabling multiple people to edit Web sites. It is a metaphor for a new era of collaboration and participation.
— Don Tapscott & Anthony D. Williams [9]

A Brief History of Collaboration

As the title suggests, this book is mainly about how to implement, use, and grow a wiki; but as the above quote makes clear, wiki technology is about more than just software; it's first and foremost about collaboration. To truly appreciate the potential for wikis, and how they can change the way we interact and share knowledge, we need a good understanding of what we mean by collaboration.

The Merriam-Webster dictionary lists several definitions for the word collaboration; however it is the first listed, and most common usage, that is perhaps the most appropriate here.

> **col·lab·o·ra·tion** \noun\
>
> 1: to work jointly with others or together especially in an intellectual endeavor.

Wikis are the epitome of a shared intellectual pursuit, as they promote a community of individuals who share an interest or a goal (sometimes both), and where sharing knowledge is central to achieving a desired result.

In his book *Wikipatterns*[5], wiki evangelist Stewart Mader suggests that "There is a special magic that happens when people collaborate. Collaboration touches on our human nature in a way that is easily felt but not so easily explained."

I am writing this introduction in my local coffee shop, and just as I finished typing the quote above, a Beatles tune started to play over the store's sound system. Is there any greater example of the benefits of collaboration than the Fab Four? One of the things I came to realize several years ago while researching the book I wrote on the Beatles' teenage years (*Before They Were Beatles*[7]), was that while collaboration between a group of people can produce great results, collaboration between particular individuals can produce remarkable results.

The band that became The Beatles went through numerous line up changes in the first six years of its existence, growing from schoolboy band to the best rock-and-roll band in Liverpool. Yet it was only when Ringo Starr and producer George Martin were added to the existing mix of John Lennon, Paul McCartney, and George Harrison, that they rocketed from local boys made good to an international phenomenon that changed a generation.

The ability and desire to collaborate is fundamental to the human condition. It was through working together that early humans developed into tribes of hunter-gatherers, and then built communities with shared dwellings and shared infrastructure. Without the drive to collaborate and learn from each other, we wouldn't be the dominant species on this planet.

As Stewart Mader points out, collaboration is a part of human nature. He says that, "when groups work together to find the best way to get a job done, the high quality of work is sustainable because they're finding the best about themselves, combining individual complimentary strengths and talents, and refining their methods at a very high level. Because they control how they work, people are more self-reflective, constructively critical of their own work, and motivated to make the best contribution possible because they take greater pride in the quality of their work."

It could be argued that to some extent the benefits of collaboration were suppressed and lost during, and since, the days of the industrial revolution and the introduction of production-line processes. As people began to increasingly focus and specialize on their particular activity, they started to lose focus on the bigger picture and how what they did affected what others in their community did. The larger overall picture became the preserve of those in power.

The true business benefits of collaborative knowledge sharing, such as improved productivity, greater efficiency, reduced cross-functional boundaries, and better access to customer feedback, have often become lost to a perceived, and in many ways understandable, fear. In the modern workplace, we have traditionally been defined, both in terms of success and hierarchy, based on what we know. The old saying that knowledge is power has been true for a long time, but the first few years of the new century have changed that.

It used to be that once someone obtained knowledge and information, they would work hard to keep that to themselves. Being known as the "go-to guy" for answers on a particular subject was a vital part of securing your position within a hierarchical structure. But, the barriers to gaining and sharing knowledge have been broken down. Internet culture, especially the social networking phenomenon of the last few years, has made knowledge-sharing the accepted norm outside of the work environment.

Today, anyone with an Internet connection has immediate access to an unprecedented wealth of information. It is possible to get the answer to almost any question in seconds with just a simple search. We expect to be able to use that information, and we expect to be able to contribute to it. The modern paradigm is that reputations are built on the knowledge that you share freely and openly. Being the "go-to" guy is no longer about what you know, it's about having the knowledge on how to apply that information.

In her book, *The New How: Creating Business Solutions through Collaborative Strategy*[6], corporate strategist Nilofer Merchant points out that "in 2010 there will be more 'millennials' than 'baby boomers' in the workforce. This new workforce will not only expect to be involved, but they will apply their talents only when they can be fully engaged."

Yet, in many companies there remains a reluctance to transfer this social behavior and desire to participate into the work environment. It is becoming clear that the accumulation and management of knowledge is moving away from the control of a few select individuals and towards a model where knowledge is the by-product of whichever communities an individual belongs to. The digital generation will expect to participate in, and leverage, this model, and that expectation will ultimately drive change.

Companies that have already embraced the idea of community contribution, such as those discussed in this book's case studies, are seeing the benefits and the increased efficiencies in the way they do business. Community-based solutions are a key element that these companies are using to build for future success.

A September, 2008, entry on the Google Docs Blog[1] was titled, *It's about communication, not the tool.* This is a sentiment I strongly agree with. However, the new age of communication also needs tools that allow collaborative communication—tools such as wikis.

---

[1] http://googledocs.blogspot.com/2008/09/its-about-communication-not-tool.html

1

Introduction

Welcome to the wonderful world of wikis. If you've picked up this book, it's probably because you already have some familiarity with wikis and want to learn a bit more about how other people have implemented and use them, or it's because you've heard the term being used and want to learn just what all the fuss is about. I hope that whichever case fits, you will find answers in the pages that follow.

What Can You Expect from This Book?

Along with advice on choosing and implementing a wiki, my aim is to help you use an organic process to grow your own wiki that will become a valuable asset rather than just another "technology fad" that is put in place but never reaches its potential.

Over the following chapters we will take a look at:

- ► What is a wiki?
- ► Deciding what you need
- ► Planning your wiki
- ► Implementing your wiki
- ► Populating the wiki and attracting the first users
- ► Choosing a wiki-gardener
- ► Keeping the wiki organized and maintained
- ► Promoting organic growth
- ► Building the community
- ► Harvesting the information
- ► User-generated content and feedback
- ► Continuous growth

At the end of the book are several case studies that highlight the ways that companies are using wikis to solve business and communication issues and improve both efficiency and customer satisfaction.

What is a Wiki and Why Should I Care?

So what is a wiki? Simply put, it's a website that anyone can edit directly in a web browser without any special editing tools or applications. With many wikis there is no special markup to learn. Editing a wiki-based website can be as easy and intuitive as using a simple word processor.

Like websites, wikis have grown to be useful in any number of ways. The potential of the wiki technology is only limited by the imagination of those who use it. What makes wikis so special is the "anyone can edit" capability, which means that development of a wiki is driven by the community of people who use it rather than an individual or a company.

Why the Model of a Static Web is Flawed

In the early days of the World Wide Web the relative simplicity of HTML markup made it easy to learn how to build and publish websites, lowering the barrier to entry and fueling explosive growth. However, most of these sites featured content that was static. That is, completed information was published to the web, but subsequent changes, additions, or corrections could only be made by the website owner. In many ways it still reflected the traditional paper model of create and publish, with just the delivery mechanism changed.

If you wanted to contribute something to the subject covered by a particular website, there were usually only two options:

1. Contact the website owner with your contribution / comments and hope that he or she would add your suggestions to the content of the site. Of course, as this was essentially a one-to-one conversation, no one else who might be interested would know about your proposed contribution. The website owner might also receive multiple messages on the same subject from different people.

2. Start your own website on the subject. Even if you linked to other sites on the subject, creating a true "web" of links among interconnected sites, anyone interested in your subject would still encounter a multitude of resources, many of which might repeat the same information or even contradict each other, with

no accessible conversation from subject matter experts on which to base any conclusions.

The wiki model allows direct editing of a web page, which enables a single website to develop into a central resource where subject matter experts can comment, challenge, and contribute within the same web page. The inherent conversation is made visible. It reduces (although will probably never eliminate) duplication of effort and in general means that the information presented is more likely to be timely and accurate.

Aren't Wikis Inaccurate?

There is a general perception that wikis, and in particular the well-known online encyclopedia Wikipedia (http://Wikipedia.org), are highly inaccurate. This is a common misconception based on the idea that if "anyone" can contribute, then the quality of data will suffer because there is no editorial control. In fact, the opposite has happened. Posted content is not subject to the whims, preferences, or even prejudices of a single editor or editorial board; it is now subject to the review of the whole community. As a consequence, other subject matter experts can comment, change, and contribute quickly and easily.

People with a passion for a particular subject tend to self-police the areas of a wiki covering that subject. They make changes very quickly, even on a public site like Wikipedia. If some misleading or incorrect information is posted (and that does happen fairly frequently), then it is often very quickly challenged and corrected.

Studies have shown that the number of "mistakes per article" on Wikipedia is actually lower than in the venerated print Encyclopedia Britannica, and that when mistakes are spotted they are corrected much more quickly online than in the printed volumes. We'll be covering the subject of content contribution and monitoring in more depth later on.

Where Do Wikis Fit with Web 2.0?

Wikis are often lumped in with other "Web 2.0" technologies like blogs, social networks, etc. This is also somewhat misleading. If you consider Web 2.0 to be defined as tools that encourage user participation, then a wiki would seem to fit. However, wikis have been around a lot longer than most of the other Web 2.0 technologies and could be considered to be a precursor for a lot of what we now consider "social media."

Although I first started using wikis on a regular basis in 2006, it wasn't until late in 2008 that I actually started to give any thought to where the technology came from and why it was called a wiki in the first place. Early on someone had told me that WIKI was actually an acronym that stood for "What I Know, Is," which, if you think about it, is a profound and philosophical statement to make about a piece of software. In fact it turns out that this definition is more of a "backronym" – an acronym applied to an existing word.

Imagine my surprise when a little research for a conference presentation on wiki implementation turned up the fact that "wiki" doesn't actually stand for anything. It isn't an acronym. In fact, wiki is the Hawaiian word for "fast."

The story goes that Ward Cunningham, creator of the first wiki site, was looking for a name to describe how quick and easy it was to set up this new style of website and remembered a counter clerk at Honolulu International Airport telling him to use the "wiki-wiki" shuttle bus.

Ward Cunningham's first wiki application, known as WikiWikiWeb or WardsWiki, was installed in March 1995 at Cunningham's object-oriented programming consulting company as a way to make the exchange of ideas between programmers easier. Although this first wiki was geared to programmers, others saw the potential and used the basic concept of online collaboration to build their own wiki engines and collaborative websites.

While perhaps the most public example of this is Wikipedia, until recently the real growth in the technology has been inside company firewalls rather than on the public World Wide Web. Many companies adopted wikis in their IT or engineering departments, somewhat mirroring Cunningham's first application, and then expanded them to other areas. (For another example see *Case Study 1*.)

With the acceptance and growth of social networks like MySpace, Facebook, and Twitter in recent years, many companies and organizations have come to realize the value of community contribution and online collaboration. Many of them have started to move some of their wiki technology from private wiki spaces behind a firewall to more open communities on the web. These examples, along with various special interest wikis, are promoting a model of user-generated content and feedback that is changing the way that companies do business.

I will be examining the concepts of user-generated content and feedback in Chapter 9, *Harvesting the Information*.

If there is one visible downside to wikis at the moment, it is that currently (late 2009/late 2010) there are so many different types of wiki software to choose from. A quick search on Wiki Matrix[11], a site that allows you to compare the functionality of various wikis, shows over 120 different wikis. In Chapter 3, *Planting The Seed – Think Before You Implement*, I will discuss how to decide which one is right for you.

Why Would You Need to Use a Wiki?

One of the most frequent questions I am asked when discussing wikis is, "why do I even need a wiki? I manage perfectly well without one." Even if you are doing everything you think you need to do, and even if you are managing those things efficiently, the odds are that you are not taking full advantage of the level of collaboration that a wiki enables.

Consider the following example:

Remembering the Alamo

My wife works for the Travis County local government here in central Texas, and one of the highlights of her job is helping to organize the county's annual History Day. Last year marked the 200th anniversary of the birth of William B. Travis, one of the heroes of the Alamo and the man Travis County was named for. When she told me about the organizational task her team had ahead of it, I suggested that they consider using a wiki to pull all the various aspects of the History Day planning together.

Unfortunately, the response from the county's IT group and others on the team was that they didn't need an online encyclopedia. They had equated the word wiki with its most famous and obvious example – Wikipedia.

Wikipedia is, of course, just one particular example of one style of implementation of one specific wiki platform and is not representative of the overall capabilities of wikis.

Remember, a wiki is a web page that anyone can edit directly in the browser without needing a separate editing tool.

So if that's all a wiki is, how could one have helped my wife's team?

Planning – Team collaboration

First and foremost, wikis are collaboration tools. Allowing members of a team to edit a shared collection of web pages provides them with a shared workspace that can easily be accessed from any computer and is visible to any team member with access rights to view the pages.

It is worth remembering that even though a wiki has the capability to be so open that literally anyone can edit it, that is rarely a good practice. Wikis work best when team members need a login and password to access the wiki, and when different permissions are set depending on each member's needs and role in the team. A well set-up and defined wiki becomes a virtual white board and meeting space.

Collecting historical data – Open to contributions from outside experts

A wiki, like Wikipedia, can be a knowledge capture and collection point. The History Day team was overloaded with documents and information on Travis that proved to be difficult to track and to consolidate. Bringing them together in a wiki space would have simplified the task. The team could have given permission to outside experts on the life of Travis and the history of the county to contribute directly to the wiki.

Drafting and reviewing material

The promotional fliers and other public documents related to the History Day were produced, like the majority of business documents, in Microsoft Word and then circulated for review. As a result the document authors had to consolidate feedback and comments from multiple reviewers, not only on the team, but from other county officials and their legal counsels.

With the documents online in a wiki, each reviewer could have either made changes directly in the document or added comments that others could have seen. By allowing all reviewers to see others' changes, duplication of effort would also be reduced.

Most wikis also have some degree of document management built into them. This means you can store different versions of the same document so you can track what changes were made and who made them. You can also control who has access to particular documents and whether they can just read them or are allowed to make changes. Using a wiki's built-in document management tools would allow any earlier version to be recreated if needed.

Collecting document scans and images for exhibits

The exhibit included many old photographs and documents, including Travis' famous "Victory or Death" letter from the Alamo, all of which had been scanned for archival purposes. Putting the electronic copies on the wiki would have allowed all members of the team to comment on which ones to use and how they should be displayed (something that was under discussion right up until the morning of the event). This might have helped create a more consistent exhibit.

Planning floor space

The floor space in the county court house allocated for the History Day event was changed this year, meaning that the team had to do some last minute reworking of where the displays would be placed. Having floor plans on the wiki would have given more time to review and think about placement instead of having to cram the decision making into one hastily convened meeting.

Directory for team, county officials, local media

A wiki is a great place to set up a contacts directory for any team, company, or organization. Each person can keep his or her own information up-to-date, and central administration is quick and easy. The directory can also add links to email clients, webpages, or even a person's home page in the wiki itself.

Easy transfer of information to county website

Most wikis use a simple markup language, called wikitext, that is easy to convert to HTML on export, and some wikis allow the use of HTML tags in their content. That way information developed collaboratively by a team on a wiki can easily be extracted and posted on a more traditional, static website.

Supplementary information for event attendees

By making parts of the wiki open to the public, attendees at the History Day event could have had access to research notes and additional information about the subject and the display items to further complement the information on the display boards.

A "playbook" to help organize next year's event

A wiki is a great way to capture procedural notes and ideas during the planning and running of an event. These can then be used in following years to review and plan for follow up events. This sort of interactive ongoing knowledge capture avoids reinventing the wheel and also makes it easier to transition new people on to the team.

Allow year-round contributions of ideas rather than a short sprint.

Traditionally, planning for this event starts a few months before the scheduled date and becomes a concentrated effort over a short period that distracts the team members from their main tasks. By keeping a project wiki available throughout the year, items could be addressed earlier and ideas contributed on an ongoing basis, making the actual planning less stressful.

Fewer meetings and no email trials.

With a well-designed wiki a lot of the collaboration that takes place in time-consuming meetings takes place online. This way it is easier for people to contribute when they have time, rather than trying to make time. Also contributors no longer have to be physically co-located or travel for planning meetings. When meetings are held, they are more productive as a lot of the preparation work has already been done online.

Holding open discussions on the wiki also decreases email traffic and helps eliminate multiple email threads where a single topic may spawn multiple parallel conversations. In fact, one of the hardest things to do in email is simply organize a meeting. Posting suggested dates and times on the wiki and having people comment there can save a lot of email traffic.

Post-event marketing.

Space on the wiki could also have been set aside for publishing photographs, press reports, and even a few "vox pop" style interviews with attendees. These would act both as a record of the event and as something that could be used to attract interest in next year's event.

By making some areas of the wiki open to the Internet, it could then be indexed by search engines. If a wiki includes a blogging feature, then search engines will tend to rank it higher in results. Once again this would attract visitors and build awareness of the event.

In short, the History Day team could have used a simple wiki as all of the following:

- ► Collaborative knowledge capture space
- ► Planning tool
- ► Content creation, editing, and review tool
- ► Document and image archive
- ► Facilities planning tool
- ► Contacts directory
- ► Publishing source for an external website
- ► Interactive media source
- ► Event planning tool
- ► Meeting planner
- ► Email replacement
- ► Marketing tool

That's a lot more than just an "online encyclopedia."

Does the scenario above sound familiar? Are you also looking for a way to increase team collaboration and manage your company's knowledge? Do you need a way to manage projects with customers or suppliers outside your company firewall? Would you like your customers to provide feedback on the information you publish?

Then a wiki might be just what you are looking for.

Perhaps you have already decided that you should use a wiki, but are not sure how to go about it. Maybe you have a wiki but would like to encourage more people to use it. Or you would just like to learn more about the practical applications for this fast growing technology.

Today's Business Challenges

Business today is a complex environment with new challenges seeming to rise on an almost daily basis. It seems that new technologies and tools appear to meet those challenges almost as fast. However, throwing new tools at new problems may not be the way to go. It may be that the best solution is to use an established technology, like a wiki, that on the face of it appears simple, yet has the flexibility to solve, or at least ease, many business operational needs.

As illustrated in the Alamo example, a wiki can bring major benefits and in some cases even replace (or eliminate the need for) several separate software applications.

But wikis aren't the answer to every business problem. The solution must match the needs of the organization and its culture.

You cannot just put up a wiki and expect everyone to start using it. The "build it and they will come" approach doesn't work, nor does mandating the use of a wiki (see *Appendix A* and *Case Study 3* for more on this topic).

Experience has shown that wiki usage, no matter what the benefit to the group may be, is inevitably an organic process. That will be the main focus of this book.

Doing it Ourselves

One question that I think needs to be addressed before going any further is, does this book practice what it preaches? I believe it does. The book was written in a wiki that was initially shared between the author, the publisher, and the cartoonist so we could work in a collaborative environment. Every person involved in the production of the book could see progress, ask questions, copy edit, and add comments at any point. Once we were at the review stage we opened the wiki up to the review team for them to further copy edit and add comments. This also allowed Scott Abel to write his foreword directly in the production wiki.

The wiki we used supports output as HTML. The team at XML Press wrote scripts to extract content from the wiki, convert it to DocBook XML, and use the XML as a single source from which they generated formatted output for both print and electronic versions of the book.

Using a wiki in this manner meant that the traditional serial production workflow for a book – complete manuscript / review & edit / format / publish – became a parallel one where reviews, editing, formatting, and test production runs could all be done while the content was still being developed. The result is a much shorter production cycle and the ability to include the latest information very close to the publication date. See *Case Study 5* for more about how this book was produced

We will also be putting the book's ideas to the test by offering a public-facing wiki where readers of this, and other XML Press titles, can comment or add information that they believe the authors, publisher, and other readers may be interested in or find useful.

You can join in the online conversation about *WIKI: Grow Your Own for Fun & Profit* at http://readers.xmlpress.net.

2

Defining the Wiki

Despite its name, and to borrow the title of a recent blog posting that made me smile, a wiki is not a character in Star Wars.

Webster's dictionary defines a wiki as "a website that allows visitors to make changes, contributions or corrections." Wikipedia defines its underlying technology as "a website that uses wiki software, allowing the easy creation and editing of any number of interlinked webpages, using a simplified mark up language or WYSIWYG (What You See Is What You Get) text editor within the browser." Just to further muddy the waters, the inventor of the wiki, Ward Cunningham, describes it as "the simplest online database that could work."

So which is it?

- A website?
- Editing software?
- A database?
- A model for collaboration and co-creation?

The truth is, a wiki is all of those things and more.

Yet, at its core a wiki is simply a website that can be edited directly in your browser without the need for any additional software.

What is a Wiki Anyway?

In his book, *The Wiki Way: Quick Collaboration on the Web*[3], wiki creator Ward Cunningham expands on his "database" statement and gives the following more detailed view of the concept of a wiki:

- A wiki invites users to edit any page or to create new pages within the wiki website, using only a plain-vanilla web browser without any add-ons.

- Wiki promotes meaningful topic associations between different pages by making page link creation easy and by showing whether an intended target page exists or not.

► A wiki is not a carefully crafted site for casual visitors. Instead, it seeks to involve the visitor in an ongoing process of creation and collaboration that constantly changes the website.

While most people associate wikis with collecting and publishing existing information, a wiki can also be used for authoring and delivering new content. From a content development and publishing perspective a wiki provides the perfect location for a group of authors and subject matter experts to collaborate. This powerful concept opens up the traditional lone author process into one where the knowledge and expertise of external contributors and knowledge holders can be quickly and easily leveraged.

Wikis are much more than a simple collection of separate webpages devoted to individual subjects. Through the addition of hyperlinks, which link pages and articles to each other, the wiki comes closer to Cunningham's vision of a database, but a database that can be easily browsed, navigated, and searched.

Wiki markup

The content of a wiki can have structure and formatting applied through the use of a simple markup language, or more commonly, through the use of a rich text editor (another name for a WYSIWYG editor). For those who prefer to use a markup language, most wiki markup is simpler than the HTML (HyperText Markup Language) used to build traditional static websites. Wiki markup languages were developed to overcome the inherent complexity of HTML, which because it mixes content and formatting markup, can be difficult to edit directly.

While there is currently no international standard for wiki markup, and different wiki developers tend to use their own variants, the basics can usually be mastered in less than an hour. However, at the time of writing most wiki software ships with a rich text editor, and it is possible to use a wiki without having to ever see an instance of the underlying markup language.

Content management

In addition to allowing users to edit content, most wikis also allow users to provide a short summary of why they made changes. This information isn't displayed on the wiki page itself, but is kept as part of the page's history and can easily be retrieved. This way it is possible to see who made changes and why. Most wikis also keep a copy of each version of a page and include a "roll back" feature that lets you restore an earlier version of the page. Some wikis also include a "diff" functionality that lets you compare two versions of a page side-by-side and see exactly where changes have been made.

This makes many wikis usable as simple content management / revision control systems, which previously would only have been possible by using separate high-cost third-party software applications.

Navigation

Navigation between the pages of a wiki is achieved through the use of hypertext links. This technique generally leads to a flat navigation structure, rather than a more formal, hierarchical structure. Links are created in wikis using a simple syntax, and it is a common practice in wikis to create a link to a page that does not yet exist in the hope that the existence of the link will encourage another participant to supply the required content for the missing page. Many wikis also include a backlink feature so you can see which pages link to the page you are currently viewing or editing.

Despite the inherently flat structure of wikis, it is still possible to create traditional, hierarchical navigation structures such as a table of contents.

The flat, some would say anarchic, format of wikis can present a management and maintenance challenge. To help with this most wikis provide ways of categorizing and tagging pages. These tags can then be used to generate sidebar lists of categories, or even a "tag cloud," a structure that displays tags in larger or smaller type depending on their relative popularity.

Studies have shown that among the "Internet generation" – those born since the beginning of the Internet in the mid-1990s – the first reaction of over 50% of users when they need to find information is to use a search tool rather than navigate through a series of steps. Wikis support this growing behavior pattern; most offer at least a title-based search, and many include full-text search capability. The performance and scalability of these searches can vary depending on whether the wiki engine uses an underlying database.

Several wikis also support the integration of third-party search engines such as Google. Understanding your search needs is critical to the successful implementation of a wiki. You may need to develop a metadata strategy to tag pages and wiki sections to assist built-in search engines, or you may need to integrate a third-party tool.

The Growth of Wikis

Wikis were initially used within enterprise-based technical communities as a collaborative software platform. Once the flexibility of wikis started to be appreciated the uses expanded, and today they are used for things such as project communication, intranets, and documentation. Many companies have totally replaced their static, HTML-based intranets with collaborative wikis. While there are still probably more wiki implementations behind corporate firewalls than on the public Internet, that landscape is also changing, with more and more wikis being made available for public use.

One example of this trend can be seen with the adoption and use of wikis by WebWorks (see *Case Study 1*).

Outside of corporations, wikis are also gaining wide acceptance and use in the consumer market. Wikipedia has become one of the most visited sites on the Internet, and for many people it has replaced textbooks as their default source of information for just about everything.

Wikis are also replacing web rings (a set of independently created, but linked websites on a similar topic) and other similar groupings of websites by special-interest groups. Instead of people with a shared interest creating their own websites (often duplicating information) and sharing cross links, these groups are now creating a wiki where people can share information in a central, searchable repository.

Wikis are also gaining popularity as individual productivity tools. A personal wiki can be used as a repository of web links or as a notepad to capture ideas and information. Some vendors offer a service that hosts your wiki on their servers. You access your wiki over the web via a login (in fact this book was written using this type of wiki). Other vendors have versions of their wikis that can be downloaded to a local machine or even run off a USB flash drive (a wiki that fits on a USB stick is sometimes referred to as a "wikiscicle," a term mentioned by Anne Gentle in her blog, *Hurdles and Hardships using Wikis for Technical Documentation*[1]). Using a wiki as a personal productivity tool has the advantage of being platform, device, and browser-independent, so you can access it and use it from any machine, anywhere.

What are Wikis Used For?

Throughout the book we will be discussing various uses of wikis across many different organizations, but the truth is that the use of wikis is only limited by your imagination. Below are some more examples of wiki uses.

For individuals

- ► Getting Things Done (GTD) productivity tool
- ► Notebook for brainstorming / idea capture
- ► Editing / content creation
- ► Project tracking
- ► Personal database
- ► Mind mapping

---

[1]   http://justwriteclick.com/2010/03/31/hurdles-and-hardships-using-wikis-for-technical-documentation/

Small groups

- Collaborative planning
- Knowledge capture
- Communication portal
- Project tracking
- Review tool

Special interest groups

- Knowledge sharing
- Collaboration
- Research tool

Company internal

- Collaboration
- Knowledge capture
- Peer review
- Database
- Official document and record storage
- Productivity tool
- Project management
- Meeting management and record keeping
- Content creation
- Content delivery

Website replacement

- Documentation online
- Conference planning
- Customer forums
- Customer support
- Image storage and retrieval
- Knowledge base
- Web portal

Large open groups

- ► Knowledge capture
- ► Collaboration
- ► User-generated content
- ► Research tool

Leading wiki consultant, Stewart Mader, editor of the Future Changes[2] blog, often cites the belief that wikis have the potential to be as ubiquitous as email is today and that in the not too distant future we will take their use for granted.

---

[2] http://futurechanges.org

3

Planting The Seed – Think Before You Implement

One of the first steps in implementing a wiki is to ask yourself the most basic question – do you really need a wiki?

You may discover that the community you are planning to set up the wiki for simply prefers another way to collaborate and communicate. One wiki I set up for a local writers group was a spectacular failure because they simply preferred to share information by having a weekly get together in a local coffee shop. The technology became superfluous to the community's needs.

However, not every company or organization can meet in the local Starbucks, so a collaboration tool that provides access and facilitates conversation across a functionally or geographically diverse group may be essential.

You must also avoid the secondary mistake we made with the writers group, installing technology for technology's sake. Though a few members of the group were techies and thought a group wiki would be cool, they didn't have a clear vision of the wiki's purpose and goals. Unfortunately nearly every case I have come across of a wiki implementation failing was due to it being a technology-driven implementation.

If you are reading this book, there is a good chance that you are what is referred to as "a technology ambassador." That is, you are among the first to look at, try, and adopt new technologies. But, be aware that the things that appeal to you as a technology ambassador can intimidate average users and even put them off using the technology all together.

So before you jump in and start, you need to think about what you are doing, why you are doing it, and how it will affect those you hope will use and benefit from the wiki.

Building the Seed Team

Ideally, you should put together a small team to help you ask and answer the questions I outline later in this chapter. The team should consist of at least:

- ► A project sponsor, champion
- ► A "techie" who has done some initial investigation into wikis
- ► An end user who represents the intended user community
- ► And ideally, an outside pair of eyes, like a consultant, who can identify ingrained communication habits and ask why certain things are done certain ways

One of the biggest worries managers, especially IT managers, have about wikis is a perceived lack of control. They may believe that wikis must be open to anyone, thus opening the door for system abuse and security risks. The opposite is, in fact, true. Most wikis offer levels of access control (sometimes to the page level) and accountability far greater than many traditional enterprise systems.

By bringing in a fresh pair of eyes, and by being free from the company's institutionalized habits and assumptions, an outside consultant can often anticipate these concerns, and help educate and manage the change more easily than an internal person can.

Even if you can't build a full "seed team" you should ask at least one other person, preferably a potential user, to act as a sounding board while you work through pre-implementation questions and concerns.

Seed Questions

Ask yourself and your team the following questions before you start, and be truthful with the answers.

Think about the issue you are trying to solve, and then see how a wiki might be applied. Remember, don't just focus on the positive, think about the potential negatives, too.

What business issue will the wiki resolve?

For any technology implementation to succeed, there needs to be a problem to be solve or an operational efficiency to be gained. Think about why you are considering a wiki. Do you have examples of wikis being used to address similar issues? Did they work? If so, why?

How will you measure success?

There are two ways you could measure success. One is by setting goals for the adoption of the wiki itself, such as measuring the percentage of the community contributing, the number of people registered, the number of new articles, or the number and frequency of comments.

The other way is to measure the wiki's success based on its impact on your business needs. For example: Did the wiki reduce the time taken for a particular process? If the wiki is a customer-facing one, how many people visited certain wiki pages? Did the wiki reduce email traffic or the number of meetings?

What is the expected return on investment?

One of the first questions asked about any new system is, "What is the financial return on investment (ROI)"? With wikis the software costs could be as low as zero for an open source solution or as high as several thousand dollars for an enterprise solution. Regardless of the software costs, the cost of populating and maintaining the wiki will probably be higher. The ROI may not be directly attributable to the wiki itself, but instead may come from a change in collaboration methodologies and operational improvements.

Before you start to consider the ROI on the wiki, you need to calculate what it actually costs you to complete certain business functions today, or how much the business issues you are trying to solve affect the bottom line. You need to know today's costs before you can calculate what you will save tomorrow.

Where will the content come from?

Meaningful content is the key to any successful wiki, so you need to think about where it will come from. While you may be looking for the community to contribute, you will most likely need to seed the wiki. Where is this initial content going to come from? Will you need to invest time in creating new content, or will you import existing legacy content, such as technical documentation, training, policies and procedures, or marketing materials? Will you need to integrate the wiki with an existing content management system? The needs of each wiki implementation will be different.

Who will use the wiki initially?

While you may be implementing a wiki to meet one particular business need, think about every area of the company, or community, that could benefit or contribute to solving that problem. Try to move beyond functional boundaries and think about the skill sets and the knowledge base of all who would benefit. In some cases this may include people located outside the organization.

Who will use the wiki in the future?

Of course, one of the great things about wikis, and the central theme of this book, is that they foster growth and further collaboration. There are numerous examples of cross-pollination of wikis inside organizations as one team sees the benefits that another has gained.

Before you start your first wiki, spend some time thinking about areas of potential growth and possible future cross-functional collaboration. Make sure you make plans for scalable growth and allow easy access for anyone who may need to contribute or observe, not just on the initial projects, but on potential future ones as well.

Who will own the wiki?

Every wiki needs a wiki maven to maintain it, something I will discuss in greater detail in Chapter 6, *Maintaining the Garden*, but it also needs someone with a sense of ownership. Be aware of inherent "not my idea" resistance in championing a wiki implementation and be prepared to give up ownership – even if the idea was originally yours – in order to ensure implementation.

Wiki branding can also be an issue. You may need to customize the look and feel of the wiki to reflect your corporate brand. Many wikis allow a sophisticated level of customization and branding, so this should not be a difficult technical issue to handle.

Where will the wiki be hosted?

The location and hosting of a wiki can be contentious and should be addressed early. In large organizations the IT group may want to host the wiki (or they may actively be against the idea). However, in certain circumstances it may be better hosted at a department or project team level or by a third party wiki hosting company outside the firewall.

Trends seem to indicate that bottom-up wiki implementations hosted by a department or project team are usually the most successful ones. In other words, it can be advantageous to "fly under the radar" in the early stages as you develop and build acceptance and usage of the wiki.

Which wiki should I use?

There are many different types of wiki in the marketplace. Don't just decide to use one type because it's the only one you've heard of. Go and do some research. Talk to people who have used wikis for similar implementations, find out what they used and why. Find out which wikis they rejected and why. Develop a short list of at least three wikis to prototype and test. See *Appendix D* for more information on selecting a wiki.

What controls will I need?

Arguably, the first rule of wikis is that there aren't any rules. It is true that wikis function best when they are driven by the communities that use them, but you need to think about a few basics of control before you start:

Do you need logins, and if so who will authorize them? Will you need to hook the wiki up to an existing user base, such as Active Directory or another LDAP store, or will it be good enough to manage the users and groups entirely within the wiki? Will you have some sort of initial structure for your wiki content?

Will you give users a "sandbox" area to learn the wiki in? Who can see, read, and edit what pages? Who will monitor recent changes and do any necessary roll backs? What's the philosophy for rolling back content and incorporating comments? You will find that these answers change and evolve along with the wiki, but it is good practice to at least set a baseline.

Answering these questions will help you build a model of expected behavior, benefits, and potential issues to be addressed before you start.

The next step is to take these answers as a baseline and start looking at both the good and the bad aspects of wiki implementation in more detail, while considering the overall question, why use a wiki?

Why Use a Wiki?

The good

- ► **Easy to set up:** Ease of setup can vary from wiki to wiki. Some can be quickly and easily set up on a desktop, or even on a flash drive for a personal edition. Setups can usually be achieved in less than an hour for personal implementations and just a few hours for a corporate version.

  Some wikis are more complex and may also require supporting tools such as an underlying database. Or you may need an IT specialist to configure the web server. Research before implementation will help you determine the complexity of the project and estimate the resources needed to meet your requirements.

- ► **Easy to use:** Navigation for most wikis is intuitive for anyone used to searching the web. Most include a search interface that returns a list of relevant pages you can then go to. In the text, links to other pages are shown using standard hypertext links, and many wikis also include a bread crumb function that shows your path from page to page. But before you implement, think about the sort of navigation needs your users may require. Look at the ways they access information.

► **Easy to edit:** Most wikis are easy to use and include a word processor-like rich text editing interface that is activated by the user clicking an "edit" button. The biggest challenge you're likely to face is a cultural one. Adopting a wiki involves change, something most humans don't like. Be prepared to teach your contributors how wikis work and why their contributions are needed.

► **Anyone can edit:** Because wikis are open and easy to use, you can allow people from all over the company or organization to contribute content and comments. Think about how this can help reduce production bottlenecks and enable collaboration and productive conversation.

► **Enables collaboration:** By lowering technical barriers to entry for new users, wikis encourage collaboration. Teams can work together to produce documents, project plans, etc. Each member of the team can easily track progress and make comments or contributions. Think about which teams may benefit from using the wiki and how you can inform and educate those teams on the benefits of using the wiki.

► **User-generated content:** Think about how much user-generated content you want in your wiki. This is one of the greatest strengths of a wiki and should be a significant factor in any wiki implementation. No one knows your product or service like your customers. They are the ones who use it every day.

By having an accessible wiki you can leverage that expertise by encouraging your customers (internal and external) to document their experiences, make suggestions, and even let you know about new ways they have found to use your product. Think about using a wiki to move publishing of product information from a one-way broadcast to a feedback loop, a conversation with your customers.

► **Tagging:** Most wikis support the use of categories and tagging, features familiar to many from Web 2.0 tools such as blogs. Think about using tags and categories as a way to provide an alternative navigation technique. Tags can replace an enforced structural taxonomy with a user-driven folksonomy based on retrieving the information users actually want, rather than what the system designers think they want.

► **Version control:** Most wikis include a version control capability, which until a few years ago would have required a separate, usually expensive, specialized third-party application. A wiki will let a user see an earlier version of a page and compare it with the current version.

You need to think about who you will let use this functionality, and what decision criteria need to be met before rolling back to an earlier version of a page. Most wikis include an optional "reason for change" field that is kept as metadata separate from the content of the page, but included as part of its history.

► **Change tracking:** Most wikis that support version control include a "Recent Changes" function that allows users to see what changes have been made, and by which user, across all or part of the wiki in a certain time frame. Think about what time frame you may want the recent changes history to reflect and whether you want to make logging a reason for change to be optional.

► **Reduced training costs:** Wiki usage is largely intuitive, and many of the skills and techniques developed in using regular word processors and surfing the web apply to wikis. However, you may need to consider short training sessions as part of the implementation process. Often this is best done in more informal sessions such as a brown-bag lunch.

The bad

While wikis are a great enabling tool with vast potential for improving many aspects of your business, they aren't perfect. Below are some of the areas of wiki usage that you need to give serious consideration to before implementation.

► **Anyone can edit:** While an open wiki encourages collaboration, anonymous editing is never a good thing. In addition, you may not want everyone to see and be able to edit everything on the wiki. Think about requiring a user login. Once you have set up a login and approval system you will be able to control access and editing rights, and if necessary you can make certain content available to particular groups of users.

While such controls can make management and control of the wiki easier, overuse can undermine the very collaborative nature of a wiki. Remember that the philosophy behind wikis is to make it easy to contribute and correct; it's better (and easier) to allow mistakes to occur, then fix them, than to try and prevent mistakes by overly restricting access.

► **User-generated content:** If not correctly organized, labeled, and managed, user-generated content can easily blur the lines between what is "official" information and what isn't. Think about how you want users to contribute and how you will manage their contributions in a controlled manner.

► **Information overload:** Wikis can grow very quickly, and if not monitored topics and pages can easily be duplicated. There may also be a tendency to overload the wiki with irrelevant information (although some might argue that nothing is irrelevant on a wiki). Consider how you will manage information, and develop some techniques for keeping it tidy.

► **Not everyone will contribute:** No matter how hard you try, you will not be able to get everyone to contribute. Some people have a natural built-in reluctance to sharing in an open forum. Consider what percentage of registered users contributing, or editing, content you think would be a benchmark for success. Look at some of the techniques described later in this book for helping people contribute, and consider which ones would work in your community.

► **Wikis need maintenance:** For a wiki to remain useful, it needs to be maintained. Maintenance tasks include user administration, cleanup, structural organization, locating or deleting orphaned pages, etc. Think about who will be responsible for wiki maintenance and how you will get the resources needed. Companies or organizations with experience maintaining a traditional, static website will find that maintaining a wiki is a lot less work, but you still need resources for maintenance.

▸ **You need to pick a wiki:** Features and functions vary from wiki to wiki. You will need to do some research to decide which wiki suits your requirements. You will also need to establish a migration path for your data in case you decide to change to another wiki format at a later date. The next section outlines several steps to help you choose the right wiki for your need.

Selecting the Right Wiki

One difficulty in selecting a wiki is that there are so many available. At the time of writing, the wiki comparison site, WikiMatrix.org[11], listed over 120 distinct wiki solutions, and the number continues to grow.

The potential confusion isn't helped by there being, as yet, no standard for the underlying markup language used by wikis to tag their content. Having said that, a contest was announced at the Balisage 2010 Markup Conference[1] for people to submit proposals for a universal wiki markup language. It will be interesting to see if a workable standard emerges, and if one does, how quickly it gets adopted.

Despite the apparent plethora of wiki choices, a few are emerging as market leaders, and it only takes a small amount of research time to establish which wikis are best suited for a particular application. (See *Appendix D* for notes on some of the more popular wiki platforms.)

Don't just jump in and implement a particular wiki because it's the only one you have heard of or because "it's the one that runs a certain famous wiki site." Consider your business needs. Look around and see what wikis other people have used to solve similar problems. Ask why they chose that solution and what alternatives they con-

---

[1] http://www.balisage.net/contest.html

sidered. Also make sure that you are not conflicting with, or even duplicating, efforts in other parts of your company.

Use comparison tools like Wiki Matrix[11] to find out if there is a user community for any of the wikis you are considering, then join and ask questions.

WikiMatrix.org provides several different ways to research and select wikis that might be suitable for your needs:

1. If you are interested in a particular wiki, then you can select that wiki from the list on the Wiki Matrix home page. You will be directed to that wiki's data page, which provides basic information such as: General Features, Systems Requirements, Data storage, Security, Development and Support, Common Features, Special Features, Linking, Syntax, Usability, Output formats and Media support. The page will also display any known security alerts, a link to a forum where you can research and ask questions, and perhaps most importantly, a listing of other wikis that are commonly compared with the one you are considering.

2. If you have a list of wikis that you wish to compare, you can simply select them from the list on the home page, click the "compare" button, and you will be presented with a side-by-side comparison.

3. The WikiMatrix site also offers a Choice Wizard[2] which will walk you through the selection and comparison process by asking a series of questions regarding required functionality.

Most wikis have free personal versions, which makes prototyping cheap and easy. Download and install several and try using them. Prototype a small project with each type and get user feedback. (See *Appendix D* to find the download sites for each wiki.)

Implementing a wiki should be viewed like any other software implementation project; lay the ground work before you start.

---

[2] http://www.wikimatrix.org/wizard.php

4

Nurturing the Seedlings

While working on this book I heard from several people who thought that various projects in their companies would have benefited from the use of a wiki to help organize information and encourage a collaborative environment. In most cases when the idea was raised the response from their IT departments boiled down to "we tried a wiki once, no one used it, so why should it be any different this time?"

Further investigation showed that in the majority of cases the previous wiki implementation consisted of installing wiki software on a server, telling people it was there, and expecting them to use it. Such failures underscore that the oft-quoted maxim about wikis – just build it, and they will come – is in fact a myth. Wiki implementation is not just a simple exercise in technology, but more of an exercise in change management and sociology.

You cannot force people to use a wiki, or any other technology solution, if it doesn't fit their needs or solve a problem for them. Just installing technology and expecting people to use it because they are told to guarantees failure. Wikis flourish through organic growth, where users see the benefit and talk about it to others.

Having said that, you may discover that the community you thought would benefit from a wiki simply prefers to collaborate and communicate in another way. As mentioned in Chapter 3, *Planting The Seed – Think Before You Implement,* a wiki I set up for a local writers group was a spectacular failure because they preferred to share information by meeting in a local coffee shop (and I can't blame them). For them, the technology was superfluous. However, not every company or organization can meet in the local Starbucks. (Ironically, this happens to be where I am sitting as I write this.)

So how do you get people to use a wiki? The most successful wikis are the ones that meet a distinct need; either they serve a specific purpose, or they improve processes and promote efficiencies. Implementing technology just because it's cool invariably leads to failure. Technology geeks (and I count myself among them) also need to realize that many of the ideas, features, and functions that get us excited and turn us into early adopters can intimidate non-geek users to the point where they are scared off and will not use a solution no matter how beneficial it may be.

There are a number of different techniques you can use to get people used to the idea of a wiki; most of the ones presented below are based on introducing a wiki in a company or team environment. You should be able to extrapolate from these and come up with similar ideas and activities based on the purpose and culture where your wiki is to be used.

One of the easiest ways to introduce the idea of a wiki is to use it for the most common (and most frustrating) group activity, organizing a meeting. How many times have you seen the following scenario play out? You send email trying to organize a meeting, and you get replies from various attendees proposing alternative schedules or asking for changes or additions to the agenda. Before long one simple email has spawned multiple email threads that have to be managed and reconciled. By posting the meeting details on a wiki and sending email pointing to the relevant wiki page, everyone involved can see any proposed changes, make comments, discuss, and quickly reach a consensus, all in one place.

Another great way to introduce potential users to the benefits of a wiki is to use it to organize a fun event, like an office party, that almost everyone will be interested in. By posting ideas for location, menu, dates, and offers to car pool on the wiki, everyone can get involved, put forward their opinions, and feel they have made a contribution to the end result.

Another example comes from a company that was contemplating an office relocation. The wiki was used to gather input from staff members as to what sort of facilities they wanted in the new space, what an ideal location would be, and what they thought about the environmental impact. Ideas for potential floor plans and layouts were posted to keep everyone informed and give everyone a voice in the process.

Using internal fun projects like this is a great way to let people experience the benefits of using a wiki without necessarily mandating its use. Once people experience the benefits, they will be more open to continued use.

Many wikis come pre-configured with templates for registered users to set up their own page and space on the wiki. Giving users their own private space is a great way to encourage wiki use. A sense of ownership is a vital part of encouraging wiki adoption and growth.

One software company uses the home page idea as a way of introducing people, not only to the wiki, but to the company itself. Every new person joining the company, whether a top-level manager or a front-desk receptionist, has to write an introductory page and blog post on the wiki on his or her first day. It's an induction task, along with "eat the chocolates that you find on your desk." They can write whatever they like. Some people post their life story, with pictures of their children and pets and favorite activities. Other people say very little.

It's a great way to get someone started at the company. Everyone reads the introductory posts, because they know what it felt like when they had to write their own. Many people add comments to the post, just saying "welcome" or chiming in and saying things along the lines of, "oh, you're a gaming fan too – join us on Thursday nights," and so on. As well as being a great welcome to the company, it gets the new person using the wiki from day one.

Finding the Initial Information for Your Wiki

Once you have people feeling comfortable using a wiki, the next stage is to seed it with even more information that is useful and relevant to the intended user community as a whole.

It may seem that the best way is to start from scratch and only load new information into the wiki once a project is underway. However, this approach will take time to develop a critical mass of information, by which point a large percentage of users may have stopped using the wiki because they "can't find anything useful."

There is undoubtedly existing content in your organization that would provide immediate benefits if imported into a wiki. But beware. When you import existing content into a wiki there is a tendency to include too much. Filling the wiki with lots of information before rolling it out can lead to users feeling overwhelmed. Early users may find it difficult to locate the information they want and consequently stop using the wiki. It will take a few iterations to get the structure and navigation scheme worked out; overloading your wiki with data at the start will only make this process more time consuming and difficult.

It is better to start with a smaller set of information and let users discover what's missing and ask for it to be included. This also gives the users the sense of owning the information because they feel responsible for its inclusion.

Selecting Information to Seed the Wiki

First look for content that every member of the community needs access to and which is updated on a regular basis. This could be project specific content, such as weekly progress reports and project time-lines, or it could be more general information such as an employee list or HR policy and procedure documents.

Also consider loading any style guides and project management documents that you regularly use.

Consider including email traffic within the community or even transcribe water cooler and hallway conversations (after you've asked the other person's permission of course!). Are there particular projects and subjects that are often discussed and debated within the team? What things spark the biggest and most sustained email threads? Consider adding background documentation with discussion pages.

And if the wiki is being set up to manage a particular project, make sure to load all the relevant project information and documents.

Whatever you choose, make sure it is information that people use. Seeding a wiki with dead information means it will remain dormant.

Importing Information into the Wiki

Once you have selected what existing information you want to use to seed the wiki, the next logical step is to import it. There are a few different approaches to tackling this problem.

Perhaps the most obvious way is to select the information you want to import and simply copy and paste it from the source documents into a relevant wiki page that you have already created. The danger in this approach, apart from the sheer tedium of the task and the time it would take, is that the word processing programs typically used to create the source information (such as Microsoft Word) embed their own hidden formatting code into the content. It may not be visible to the user, but it stays with the content. The chances are that this hidden formatting will not be suitable for online presentation in a wiki. So you will need to clean up any imported text by examining the underlying source code.

Instead of cutting and pasting, another possibility would be to retype the information you need directly into the wiki. Again, this would be a tedious and time consuming operation, which also increases the risk that mistakes will be introduced into the copied information. To prepare the retyped information for presentation online, you would then have to manually apply formatting through the use of the wiki's rich text WYSIWYG interactive editor or via the manual application of wiki mark-up code.

Another option for importing existing content into the wiki: upload the original documents to the wiki just as they are, and attach them to the wiki pages. Some wikis can display the content of attached files directly on the wiki page, provided the file is one of the supported types (usually PDF, Microsoft Word, Excel and PowerPoint). This means that people viewing the content can view it directly on the web, without needing to have Microsoft Office installed on their computers. It also means that you can postpone converting the content to the native wiki format until you need it as such.

In some cases the whole import process for populating a wiki can be automated by using commercial content conversion tools. There are several available that will convert from one specific content format to one specific wiki (for example, from Word to Confluence). Some vendors offer products that convert content from a variety of sources, (or even combined from different sources) to a selection of the most popular wiki platforms. These more sophisticated tools often include features to predetermine design features, structure and even navigation aids.

When setting up a new wiki and pre-populating it, there can be a tendency to overload it with information to the extent that, as mentioned earlier, it can both confuse and intimidate the new user.

Wiki Markup

Wiki markup is often considered to be one of the biggest barriers to wiki adoption, yet this is something of a myth that persists from the early days of the technology. The first wikis used a markup language that used simple, one or two character tags around a section of text to make it display in a particular way. For instance, instead of using the HTML bold tag (bold), a wiki might surround the text with two underline characters (__bold__).

The problem was, and still is, that there was no standard for wiki markup language. The need to learn a new markup language for each wiki is seen by many as an insurmountable problem. In most cases this is little more than an excuse since most wiki markup is simple and logical and can be learned in around an hour.

As wikis matured and their use expanded beyond software developers, who are used to markup languages, wiki markup started to be replaced by more familiar word-processing interfaces where formatting is applied by keyboard short cuts or menu items and buttons on a tool bar. Now the vast majority of wikis ship with word processor functionality, and users don't need to learn the underlying wiki markup.

Creating the Initial Navigation and Hierarchies

Do not try and impose a complex hierarchy on the information at first. Start with an open, flat structure that will allow users to develop their own hierarchies as they work with or add content. It will not take long before a natural community-driven navigation model will emerge that reflects the way people actually work and organize information. This community-driven structure will require management and house keeping, which I will discuss in more detail later.

A traditional, imposed structure based on what someone thinks you should be doing, rather than what you actually do, can lead to frustration and is contrary to the open model of a wiki. By its very nature a wiki should reflect the nature and needs of the community.

However there may be instances where the business need calls for a strictly imposed structure, or where the nature of the community is such that it would be happier, at least at the beginning, with some sort of enforced structure. The trick is to balance the needs with the capability of a wiki and the benefits it can bring. The great thing about wikis, is that you can, if necessary, remodel and rearrange the structure to reflect the communities needs and behavior over time.

For many, the basic book paradigm is the most familiar and comfortable organizational method. It seems natural that we should navigate using structured tables of content and indexes. However, this doesn't reflect the way more "digitally aware" people work.

No matter what progress we make in other areas, when it comes to information sharing and delivery we are still obsessed with old ways of thinking. The advent of digital information delivery, such as wikis and eBooks, is being heralded as a revolution in thinking, but I'd argue that often the technology is just a shiny new package for the same old ideas. We are still locked into a book-based, page-locked paradigm that has changed little since the dawn of the printing press. Today most eBooks are little more than simple electronic page turners, built for, and largely consumed by, tech-savvy, gadget-loving members of the older generation (among which I count myself.)

But this model will not work for the new generation of information consumers.

Those of us raised on more traditional media (i.e. the printed word) are most comfortable with a book paradigm where information comes in a structured format (chapters with headings and sub-headings), and navigation is either a map to that structure (a table of contents), or an alphabetical listing of subjects (an index).

Naturally, when we started to deliver information electronically we carried that paradigm over. Sure we made a few concessions to the new media, but the underlying print-based model stayed, because that's what we were comfortable with. It's what we naturally understood, and it matched the way that we handled locating and using written information outside of the work environment.

How a new generation navigates

Helping my teenage daughter with a school project on Pearl Harbor made me realize that the new generation now entering the workforce has a completely different way of accessing information.

To research her project, the first thing she did was go to Google, search for "Pearl Harbor" and start visiting links. Her first stop was Wikipedia.

Then she got on Facebook and YahooIM and started using messaging to ask friends who were online for recommendations. These friends were literally from all around the world, including a family friend in Japan, so she was given access to resources that gave totally different perspectives from those given in the classroom and local school board approved text books. As I watched, she soon had six different windows open on her iMac and was pulling information from multiple sources into her own document, interactively building the structure and narrative as she went.

One friend suggested going to a social bookmarking site and searching using a variety of user-applied tags. Instead of being driven by a pre-defined taxonomy she was now applying a community-derived folksonomy.

Of course being a bibliophile and a bit of a history geek, I had a few good old-fashioned print books on World War II sitting in my home office. I proudly placed them on the edge of my daughter's desk and suggested she look through them for information on Pearl Harbor, too.

She dutifully picked up a couple of the books and started flicking pages over, skimming through the contents.

"Why don't you use the Table of Contents or Index?" I asked.

"That just confuses me. I can find stuff quicker this way," she replied, looking in bemusement at her obviously aged father.

I sat back and watched her navigate the books for a few minutes. She quickly found what she needed – and then I realized what she was doing. She was "browsing" just as if she was online.

That's when I started to question the paradigm that has informed the way I've thought about information delivery for over two decades. The book-driven, structured paradigm may have been ideal for my generation, but what about the new generation?

Since that moment of realization I have continued to watch and learn how people use today's technology to access information and tried to extrapolate from that what they will expect in the not too distant future.

For kids raised as part of the digital generation, where the first place they go to find out information is the Internet and social networks, the book paradigm is becoming irrelevant. In most cases trying to build a wiki using the book paradigm is not the best approach. Wikis are not designed to be accessed and read in a linear sequential manner, so we shouldn't set one up based on that model.

Of course, like anything with wikis, there are exceptions, and there will be cases where setting a wiki up to replicate the book model may be the right solution (such as the wiki used to write this book).

If most of the user community is happier finding information via a search, or via categories and tags, then the wiki should reflect that.

Design for the Culture, not the Process

Do not model the initial wiki structure on an existing process, whether it's paper or electronic. Wikis function best when they grow organically in response to the culture of the group using them.

Implementing a wiki is a great time to ask the most often overlooked question when it comes to process – "Why?" as in "why do we do that?" If the answer is, "we've always done it that way," then keep asking. It is likely that something implemented for a culture that existed in the past no longer applies to the current culture.

You will also need to do a periodic review to see if the content needs to be reorganized to accommodate changes in business goals, the team structure, or even the personality mix of the team members. Remember, a wiki will be a reflection of the community, and as the community evolves, so must the wiki.

Before you start, think about the way your team actually operates and interacts, rather than the way the company procedures say it should.

- ► Is your company a formal hierarchical organization or a loose interactive one?

- ► Is there already a history of collaboration, or is your traditional workflow constrained by functional boundaries?

Social Reinforcement

Social reinforcement can be a powerful tool for encouraging wiki adoption and usage. If a hallway discussion generates a great idea or observation, instead of ending the conversation with "send me email with that," consider saying, "put that on the wiki so everyone can take a look and comment." Such an approach removes the email "black hole" where the sender is never sure if the recipient acted on ideas. After someone has posted something useful, verbal feedback, even just a quick "nice wiki post," can make the poster feel that his or her contributions were read and valued.

It is also important that the people implementing and encouraging the use of the wiki are seen to be active participants. Asking others to use something that you don't use yourself is a sure recipe for failure. Senior managers who want to promote a wiki must participate themselves. A wiki will only succeed if key stakeholders and sponsors participate.

Wikis are by their nature a social network, and like all social networks they grow and function best through recommendations. Collect stories about how wikis make it easier for people and teams to deliver on their objectives. Encourage people to share those stories. "I found that on the wiki" should become a catch phrase within your community.

Setting Expectations for Participation

One of the biggest reasons for implementing a wiki is that it is a shared editing environment; with that comes an expectation that the community will participate by adding, commenting on, or editing content. But beware, when you implement a wiki you must have realistic expectations of the level of user activity and contribution.

At the start of this chapter I mentioned the typical IT department response that "no one used it." But, what exactly do they mean by "no one," and what level of activity were they expecting? In most cases little thought is given to the expected level of participation before a project starts. This can doom the project to failure.

The truth is that participation levels vary considerably, and you should set your expectations accordingly. The more bounded the community, the more likely you are to see higher participation levels. This is especially true for wikis inside a corporate firewall. One small specialist software company reports that they have had at least one contribution for their internal wiki – a company intranet replacement – from 90% of their employees, and active participation is at around 50%. A company that used a wiki for one specific business project saw participation from around 35% of the staff.

Outside the firewall, numbers are lower; a large international non-profit I talked to saw participation from around 12% of their global staff and considered that a great success. With open public wikis, such as Wikipedia, or product documentation wikis, the participation figures can be orders of magnitude lower. In her book *Conversation & Community: The Social Web for Documentation*[4], Anne Gentle describes the 90-9-1 rule, which postulates that for every 100 visitors to a public wiki, 90 will be just readers, nine will contribute something, and just one will be an active contributor.

Setting an expectation on the level of participation based on industry experience can help determine realistic goals for any wiki implementation acceptance criteria.

5

First Growth

Structure or Chaos?

One of the first questions asked when implementing a wiki is how to set up a structure for the information it will contain. There is a common belief that the inherent open nature of a wiki will inevitably lead to chaos. In some senses this isn't too far off the mark, so perhaps the best question to ask when deciding on a wiki structure is how much chaos can your community tolerate.

Remember, the decisions on usability, navigation, and structure will come from the community. The looser the structure you start with, the more likely it is that an efficient usable structure will evolve. Force fitting a structure, your own or a traditional company model, will limit the effectiveness of the wiki and rob it of much of the value that comes from a collaborative community environment.

Those of us raised on more traditional media (i.e., the printed word) are most comfortable with the book paradigm where information comes in a structured format, like chapters with headings and subheadings, and where navigation is either a map (a table of contents) or an alphabetical listing of subjects covered (an index).

Naturally, when we started to deliver information electronically we carried that paradigm over. We made a few concessions to the new media, but the underlying print-based model stayed because that's what we were comfortable with. It's what we naturally understood, and it matched the way that we handled locating and using written information outside of the work environment. However, this model no longer works for a new generation, which has always known and used the Internet and which has developed a different way of accessing information. This generation has a much looser way of searching for and accessing information that abandons the hierarchical book structure for one based on searching, peer recommendation, tagging, and browsing.

We need to bear these differences in mind when designing the wiki's structure. What makes a wiki uniquely valuable is that it will develop organically, based on the needs of the community, and will create its own folksonomy rather than adhere to an imposed taxonomy.

A model based on the book paradigm may not be instinctive and can easily lead to confusing navigation paths. Also, the book paradigm can lead you to base the wiki on the existing source document hierarchy and navigation schema, rather than allowing the content structure to develop organically. By applying an existing structure you could be limiting the potential for a community-driven schema without even realizing it.

As I stated earlier, a degree of chaos is inevitable in the early stages of any successful wiki implementation. The question is, how much chaos is the community willing to tolerate?

Whatever level of chaos you decide you can tolerate, you need to develop a management approach that supports it. In the early stages of developing this book I posted the following note on Twitter:

"The first rule of wiki is that there are no rules."

While many agreed with this sound bite, some objected. The idea of total chaos and freedom of input was contrary to their nature and culture. In such cases you may want to create an initial minimum structure so that you have some guidelines for contributors.

In practice, the majority of groups will prefer at least some basic guidelines and templates to a totally open system. This sort of implicit governance builds trust in both the wiki and the content. Self-governance also encourages good behavior within the community.

Be aware that the structure your community needs may not be the one that you think it needs. Whenever you enforce even a minimal structure make sure to monitor it for emerging patterns and be prepared to adjust accordingly.

In his excellent book, *Wikipatterns*[5], Stewart Mader discusses and catalogs many of the different types of behavior that wiki contributors develop and use during a wiki implementation. By studying and recognizing these patterns you can quickly make necessary design and structural changes

Wikis are Content-driven, not Layout-driven

In publishing, information tends to presented in one of two ways: layout-driven or content-driven.

Layout-driven design applies more to traditional magazine, newspaper, and book markets where the content is often trimmed and rearranged to meet the physical constraints of space.

Content-driven design applies to more general documentation, such as legal papers, technical manuals, etc., where space is less of a consideration, and the information itself is paramount. In these cases there tends to be an ongoing flow of text, and the space expands to accommodate the required content rather than restricting it.

Wikis are content-driven.

It seems that the best way for a wiki to develop is to adopt what I term an "open space" model; that is, let users post what they want, where they want, and let the structure develop itself. However, this approach is not without issues.

- ► Firstly, the idea of such a chaotic model can be daunting to people used to a more formal structure

- ► Secondly, this approach can lead to issues such as orphaned pages and duplication of information

Where you have an open space wiki model you need someone, a wiki-maven, dedicated to maintaining and managing the wiki and its content. The most successful wikis adopt the open space model and develop active communities.

First Steps – Personal vs. Company Approach

Having decided that you need a wiki, and having developed an approach for structuring the information, how do you go about getting people to actually start contributing content?

Earlier in the book I discussed the idea of using a "fun" project to get people using the wiki and becoming accustomed to its features, functionality, and benefits. This is certainly a proven, viable approach, but what if there are no projects that fit that model? Is there an alternative approach?

One approach I would recommend is the personal one. Today almost everyone is familiar with the concept of having a home page in social network applications like Facebook to post information, photographs, etc. When setting up a wiki, set up a "homepage" template and a few examples individuals can use to create their own environment. Giving each person an area on the wiki provides a safe place to experiment and get used to editing and contributing.

Some things people might want to put on their home page include:

- ► a photograph
- ► a short professional bio
- ► a list of skills and qualifications
- ► office location
- ► contact information
- ► schedule information
- ► links to external personal websites

A professional, corporate wiki home page is not a substitute for Facebook or other external social networks, so posting holiday snaps, pictures of the dog, etc., may not be appropriate. What is deemed appropriate will, as with other aspects of the wiki, be determined by the culture of the community. You should not dictate what should be included; remember that a homepage is personal space.

A home page could just as easily apply to a project group, a department, or any grouping of the community that you want. But always remember that the contributors to your wiki are individuals, and allowing them a sense of individual identity will lead to a sense of involvement and ownership.

The idea of a home page and the "fun" project are not mutually exclusive, and they aren't the only two methods for encouraging users. You can, and should, mix and match techniques. Experiment. Try different ideas and see what does, and just as importantly, what does not, resonate with the wiki community. Don't try just one technique and then abandon the wiki because it didn't work. It takes a while to build a critical mass of content users and contributors.

Sustaining Growth – Encourage, Don't Mandate

Encouragement is also a viable methodology for creating and sustaining wiki usage. I am often asked how to encourage someone to use a wiki. As with any change, you must be genuine in your motives. Simply mandating a wiki when you don't really care, or when you know there is no cultural acceptance of the potential benefits, will lead to failure.

There isn't a single encouragement technique; as with other aspects of wiki implementation, it is more about sociology than technology. Different techniques work best with different people and personality types. The truth is that you often need to use a combination of different methods to produce the best results. However, the one overriding truth is that a sense of enthusiasm and involvement from the people advocating the use of the wiki is essential.

Peer encouragement is perhaps the most effective. Experience has shown that wiki growth in the early stages can be exponential as others see the benefits being gained by early adopters. The rate of growth will slow as the percentage of contributors reaches its natural level for the given community. However, the influence of peers can help spread the use of the wiki into other functional areas.

Verbal feedback is one of the simplest and most effective ways to encourage wiki usage. A verbal acknowledgment that someone has posted something on the wiki reinforces that person's sense of worth within the community. This sort of feedback is also often overheard by other potential contributors and can add to the sense that they too should be adding to the wiki.

Verbal reinforcement can be used with other recognition techniques, such as mentioning a contribution during a team meeting, or sending a short "nice article" email. This sort of activity builds a recognition that the effort of adding things to the wiki not only helps the individual, but also the community as a whole. In some cases, such as a software user community wiki, you may want to recognize frequent and quality contributors by bestowing some special title or rank on them, such as an "MVP" award. This can then be seen by other users as a goal to aim for and may encourage greater participation.

Another great way to get people to participate is by providing visual feedback on wiki activity in a place that all potential contributors can easily see.

Some ideas include the following:

- ► Publish statistics on wiki usage in the form of charts that can be shared at team meetings, posted on bulletin boards, or shown to senior management to get their buy-in if necessary.

- ► Post screenshots showing recent activity or latest updates. Select a time when something interesting or relevant to the team as a whole has been added. Print it out and display it on a notice board. This can have the effect of making people who haven't yet contributed feel that they are missing out on something valuable.

- ► Display a list of the most commented on posts on the front page. This encourages comments and stimulates debate.

- ► Select a post to be the "post of the week," or something similar, and display it on the wiki home page. This instills a sense of pride and ownership.

The best way to get people to use and contribute to a wiki is to do it yourself, and not just at the start. Your commitment must be on-going. If users see the person responsible for the wiki stop using it, then they will too. There really is no substitute for "monkey see, monkey do." Leading by example is still the best way to get other people to participate.

Don't Let Go – Keep Reminding Them

Reinforcement through repetition is another way to get people to use a wiki. Once you declare that the wiki is the preferred place for certain activities and content, then you need to stick to that process.

This means that at the start you may sometimes have to take things sent to you in email and transcribe them on to the wiki. However, making "put it on the wiki" a repeated refrain within your community will eventually make the wiki the automatic destination for information. This also has the side benefit of drastically reducing the contents of your email inbox.

Up to 60% of business documents just end up sitting as email attachments (many unopened). Putting things in one central place on a wiki makes it easier to find them. It also makes it easier to recover information, since your wiki should be backed up.

If you use the maxim that "if it's not on the wiki it doesn't exist," it will make the wiki the default place of record, and usage and contribution will follow.

6

Maintaining the Garden

Identifying the Gardener

One of the most frequent excuses I hear for not implementing a wiki is that they need maintenance. To be honest, this is a response that I find bemusing. All software systems need maintenance. Be it a large complex enterprise system or even a word processor on your laptop, you still need to make sure that updates are applied on a regular basis, that information is backed up, and that directory structures are maintained. No matter what the software or IT solution is, if you just install it and leave it, then you will eventually have problems.

The same rules apply to any data set that is used and accessed on a regular basis. Be it a large database or a simple financial spreadsheet, it will need someone to monitor, update, and maintain it. Wikis are no different.

Unfortunately, historically a lot of wikis have been installed and implemented with a "set-up and forget" attitude with little or no thought given to ongoing maintenance. Finding someone to tend the wiki and developing a maintenance schedule are essential parts of the implementation process.

You need a wiki-gardener.

In some organizations this person is referred to as a wiki-maven or even a wiki-ninja. Employ whatever title or phrase works best for your community.

The ideal gardener for your wiki needs to be someone who is passionate about the wiki and its aims. He or she needs a clear understanding of your business needs, but must also empathize with the users and their needs. Often you will find technical writers have the right attributes for this role as they have the required skill set and are able to balance technical needs, usability, information design, and navigation.

The Gardener's Tasks

In addition to general system maintenance, content will need to be weeded, which includes monitoring for things such as orphaned pages, duplication of content, or an unbalanced structure.

One of the great advantages of a wiki is that you can easily add a link to a page that doesn't yet exist, but that you believe needs to be added at some point. However, over a period of time you need to monitor these empty links to determine if they are really necessary. You may find that the subject has already been covered on another page, and you need to merge the pages.

Given the open nature of a wiki, it is also possible that two or more people may create separate pages on identical, or closely related, subjects. (This is more likely to happen in the early days of the wiki implementation before the user community becomes fully familiar with the navigation and search model of the wiki.) As part of the maintenance process you need to monitor, and where necessary, merge duplicated pages.

In the early days of wiki implementation you may also find that the initial structure that you outlined (if you outlined any) becomes unbalanced. This can also happen in a totally open wiki where the structure grows organically. An unbalanced structure is one where certain articles and pages develop multiple, nested sub-pages while others remain as single pages with no attached hierarchy. When sketched out, such a structure will appear to have some areas where it is totally flat and others areas with a fairly complex hierarchical structure. In some cases you may need to move pages around to create a more balanced structure and improve navigation.

Scheduled Maintenance

Wiki maintenance, like any good maintenance (such as on your car), needs to be scheduled and completed at regular intervals. And like car maintenance, you can't do everything at once, you need to schedule different tasks at different times.

Here is a suggested wiki maintenance schedule.

Daily

- ► Check recent changes
- ► Check and review comments

Weekly

- ► Collect usage statistics

Monthly

- ► Review for orphaned pages
- ► Analyze usage statistics and trends

Quarterly

- ► Check structure
- ► Audit navigation

This is only an outline, and you may find you need to add additional tasks to the list or change the priority and frequency of various tasks.

Developing a Sense of Ownership

Above all, your wiki-gardener needs a sense of ownership.

Ideally the gardener should be involved in the early stages of the wiki project and have a stake in its success. He or she needs to understand the business aims of the wiki, why it is there, what the perceived benefits are, and what the criteria for success are. Your gardener must also be a trusted member of the user community.

In many cases the person responsible for the wiki is the original wiki champion, although in larger organizations this isn't always possible. It may be that the maintenance of the wiki falls under a different functional department, such as IT, in which case the potential wiki-gardener needs to be invited into the project team as early as possible.

Don't just appoint a wiki-gardener as if it were just another check list item on the project plan. You need to find a person with both a technology background and an ability to interact with users.

It also helps if you develop a sense of ownership among the contributors or subject matter experts for selected areas of the wiki. Spreading ownership makes maintenance easier.

Ben Allums, Director of Engineering at Quadralay, an Austin, Texas-based software company, has developed what he terms the "tennis ball" theory of wiki ownership, in which he postulates that content without an owner will stay untended in the wiki and will get moved around with no real sense of its inherent value.

The name for his theory comes from a story he tells about how an early employee at the company was a regular tennis player who was in the habit of bringing tubes of tennis balls into the office. At some point one of these tubes of tennis balls ended up in the server room, and there it stayed. Even long after that employee had left the company, people just kept moving the tennis balls around from one shelf or rack to another without ever questioning why they were there in the first place.

In the end the tennis balls survived several server room reconfigurations and even a couple of company relocations. The tennis balls stayed in the company for almost 14 years! Even though they patently had no value or contribution to the function of the server room, no one asked, "why is that there, what is it contributing," and perhaps more importantly "who owns these tennis balls?"

With wiki content it is vitally important to ask these questions:

- ► Why is this content here?
- ► What is it contributing?
- ► Who owns this content?

At first it would seem logical that the owner of the content should be the person who first contributes the topic or suggests the page, since that person obviously saw a need for that particular piece of information to be added to the wiki. However, this may not always be the case. It may make more sense to set up a page and then hand over ownership to a subject matter expert.

Another skill that the wiki gardener needs to develop is conflict resolution. Due to the collaborative nature of wikis it is possible, although relatively rare, for online conflicts to arise. These can include the following:

- ► Disagreements in a comments thread about a wiki post.

- ► Dueling edits where one person makes an edit, someone else changes that edit, and the two then go back and forth repeatedly changing each other's edits back to their own preferred version.

The wiki gardener needs to establish protocols for when to step in and resolve conflicting comments and may need to limit how many back and forth edits to allow before investigating. He or she also needs to identify trigger points for when to take conflict resolution off line, talk to the individuals personally, and in extreme cases escalate the issue to a manager.

During a wiki's growth you may find it necessary to reallocate the ownership of various pages as the structure develops and usage patterns emerge; this is a natural consequence of a wiki's organic development.

Ownership does not mean that only the designated owner can edit the page; that would defeat the collaborative underpinning of any wiki. However, the designated owner is responsible for the upkeep and monitoring of various pages, leaving the wiki-gardener free to look after the needs of the wiki as a whole.

7

Landscaping

No matter how well you think you have modeled the initial design of your wiki, the simple truth is that you will need to redesign it, perhaps several times, before you settle on a configuration that meets most of your needs. In fact, you may never actually reach an optimum wiki configuration; like any well tended garden, your wiki may never be complete. There will always be something you want to do, and you just have to balance the level of effort with the perceived benefit of the work.

In Chapter 6, *Maintaining the Garden*, we discussed the need for a wiki-gardener; someone who will maintain the wiki and keep it tidy. By definition, tasks such as upgrades, merging duplicate pages, and tracking orphaned pages are more akin to the regular weeding we all do (or to be strictly accurate, that my wife does) in our gardens. However, just like a regular garden, there will be times when to keep a wiki growing and appealing you need to undertake a landscaping project.

Not only will user behavior determine new navigation paths, it will also determine structure. As the wiki continues to develop it will change to reflect the wishes and the behavior patterns of the community. Where people place content may not align with the original ideas and plans of the implementers. The structure of a wiki will never remain fixed. As different contributors and users join the community, a structure that reflects their interests and ways of working will emerge and continue to evolve. There is really no point at which you can declare that an active wiki is "finished" or "frozen."

Even the most open and flat wikis have some basic structure when they are first implemented. Even when you strive for an environment driven through folksonomy, there will inevitably be a degree of applied taxonomy at various stages during a wiki's growth and development.

When a wiki has been established for a while, the users will begin to develop their own structure and navigation paths, and distinct patterns of behavior will emerge. It would be very rare indeed if these behavior patterns matched the original design.

It is like laying an aesthetically pleasing garden path and then watching all the kids take a short cut across your manicured lawn, you know that at some point the best thing to do will be to give up and move the path to match the route that people naturally use to get from one side of the lawn to the other. It is the same with a wiki – there will be a time when you have to face a landscaping project.

A wiki landscaping project may include things like:

- ► redefining the structure
- ► moving pages around
- ► creating tagging categories
- ► building a navigation pane
- ► rearranging pages and links

When to Start Landscaping

Undertaking any type of redesign work on a wiki is not a project to be undertaken lightly, and deciding when it is due is an imprecise art. Recognizing when to redesign is, like so many aspects of wiki management, as much a function of social observation as it is of technology and metrics. The only true indication that a redesign is necessary is increasing frustration of the wiki users. But if you leave the decision until that stage is reached, it may be too late.

Some of the signs to look for include the following:

- ► a noticeable and measurable drop-off in activity, easily spotted through daily checks on the wiki's Recent Changes page

- ► an increase in cries of "I can't find it anymore" when searching for particular content

- ► a trend of people avoiding the wiki, storing information on individual desktops, and sharing information through email

While these are good indicators of increased user frustration, you should never wait for things to reach this level before taking action. From the first day of implementation watch what your users are doing, see how they interact with the wiki, and look at how they search for and find information. Monitor the ways that they contribute. Watch how they navigate.

You don't need expensive formal usability tests, although in larger implementation projects this may be useful, but you can watch informally, listen to comments about people's experience, and ask for feedback. By establishing your own constant feedback channel you can spot trends and potential roadblocks before they appear.

Web analytics tools can also be used to spot trends in usage. These tools can show you which pages are the most popular, and just as importantly which pages never get looked at. Web analytics can also help track traffic patterns through the wiki.

Planning and making the necessary changes to the wiki before minor inconveniences grow to high levels of frustration will help ensure continued growth and use of the wiki. If you wait for the frustration level to grow to critical levels, you can enter a cycle of rebuilding that will only deliver diminishing returns and an increasing workload.

Recognizing and Exploiting Wikipatterns

In his excellent book *Wikipatterns*[5], leading wiki evangelist and consultant Stewart Mader describes how observed, repeated methods of behavior can be described as "wikipatterns." On the Wikipatterns website[12], these behaviors are grouped as either people patterns or adoption patterns (remember what I said about wiki adoption being as much a sociology exercise as a technical one?).

At the time of writing there are over sixty different wikipatterns listed on the website.[1] Each wikipattern has its own wiki page, which includes the following information:

- ► A definition
- ► A usage example
- ► Links to related patterns
- ► Suggested further reading

---

[1] http://wikipatterns.com

► A comments thread

It is well worth familiarizing yourself with these wikipatterns so that you will be able to recognize and predict them.

You should also familiarize yourself with wiki anti-patterns, that is, behavior that is detrimental to the usage and growth of the wiki. Examples include Wikiphobia, Over Organizer, Design By Committee, Too Much Structure, etc. Many of these are also listed on wikipatterns.com.

When it comes to landscaping your wiki, focus on the wikipatterns for navigation and organizing content. By observing the way that people place content on the wiki, or navigate around it, you will be able to determine where to locate content, or how to set up navigation techniques that work for your community. You may need to set up a combination of wikipatterns and navigation techniques.

I have seen one software company wiki that successfully combines three different navigation techniques, each designed to meet the needs of one part of the company's diverse customer base:

1. A traditional collapsible, tree-structure Table of Contents pane was created at the left-hand side of each wiki page for those users who are more comfortable navigating through a traditional book-based online help model.

2. A series of category type labels was created for those users who are comfortable with the social network-driven paradigm of tagging pages that interest them. These pages can then be grouped and searched by a category type, even if there is no direct structural relationship between them. Having a pre-defined category list that users can easily see (and add to) reduces the need to accommodate synonyms.

   For instance, users are considerably less likely to create labels such as "airplane," "aeroplane," "plane," "planes," etc., if there is already a clearly defined label of "aircraft" available to use. These category tags can then be used to create visual navigation aids such as tag clouds or to generate a "related pages" list of all the other pages labeled with the same tag.

3. A page of wiki "permalinks" (with its own permanent link from the wiki's home page) lists and assigns permanent links to the most popular pages. For a corporate internal wiki, that could be links to things like an employee directory, the HR policies & procedures, etc. In a product documentation wiki, that could be links to things like a "quick start" page. The permalink process is used to create a unique, unchanging reference to a specific version of an article on the wiki.

Ownership and Control

As technical communications industry blogger, Tom Johnson, points out (I'd Rather be Writing: Organizing Content, 6/3/2010[2]), part of the problem of organizing content on wikis is a perceived lack of control. Johnson says, "as soon as a wiki becomes a collaborative effort, with multiple authors, the organization becomes much more challenging and is likely to suffer from inconsistency and chaos." He cites the WordPress Codex,[3] a wiki for users and developers of the WordPress blogging software, as an example where some information is grouped together under logical headings, while other information is not.

Johnson then goes on to discuss the use of categories and subcategories as a way of marking information within wikis. This can be a very useful technique, but, as Johnson cautions, you need to define what a category is and how it should be used, because mislabeling can lead to a taxonomy that is just as confusing as the wiki structure problems you were trying to solve.

To avoid such instances you may need to develop labeling guidelines. Sun Microsystems has published specific guidelines for labels and categories in *Writing in the Open: Using Wikis to Create Documentation*[8].

---

[2] http://idratherbewriting.com/2010/06/03/from-help-authoring-tools-to-web-tools-especially-wikis-organizing-content-12/

[3] http://codex.wordpress.org

To quote Ben Allums of Quadralay again (Scenes from the Engine Room: How to keep your Wiki Growing, 4/2/2009[4]), there are three pillars that can be used to support any sustainable wiki: ownership, tagging, and permalinks. If you are missing any of these, consider adding them as part of your redesign.

While tagging and permalinks are to some extent technical solutions, the idea of ownership is more of a sociological one. By definition, with a corporate wiki, contributions will come from people in different departments or functional groups. It's a matter of human nature that departments and teams will "protect their turf" to demonstrate how they are adding value to the organization. Therefore, departmental ownership encourages teams to create barriers to knowledge sharing and build hierarchical structures.

The key is to move ownership of wiki pages from a functional or departmental level to a personal level. If a subject matter expert contributes on a regular basis to certain pages, ask that person to take ownership of those pages. You may find that people have interests and skills outside their functional responsibilities and will be willing to take ownership of other areas of the wiki that interest them. For instance, if you use the WikiMatrix[5] site, you will notice that the data page for each wiki type gives you the name of the person who "owns" that page, with a link to his or her profile page. Using this technique makes the wiki more personal.

Reorganizing Content

Once you have recognized the patterns of behavior and usage that indicate that a reorganization of content may be necessary, what must you consider before tackling such a project?

Once you have decided that a redesign is necessary and have considered any new techniques you want to use, how do you go about making these changes? The one thing you don't want to do is to just jump in and start making ad-hoc changes in the existing wiki.

---

[4] http://blogs.webworks.com/allums/2009/04/02/how-to-keep-your-wiki-growing
[5] http://wikimatrix.org

Set-up a "sandbox" area of the wiki, or better yet, a separate test bed wiki, where you can import some of the existing data and experiment with your ideas. Move information around, add categories and tags, build navigation schemes, etc. But, do it in a secure location where only a few people have access and where your activities will not affect the current wiki.

As you try out new ideas, make sure to test them. Once you are satisfied, gradually open the test-wiki up to a wider audience of trusted users and gather their feedback and input. Make more changes, then test and refine until you are confident that the changes you have made will both continue to meet your business needs and improve the experience for users of the existing wiki. Don't change for the sake of change – whatever you do must be done with the aim of both meeting the needs and behavior of the existing community and attracting new users.

It may not always be necessary to try out your redesign on a sandbox first. It depends on the scale of the redesign and the nature of the material. If you're just tagging pages and then using the tagging to design a structure, then you're not materially affecting the content. It's metadata. So you could build it on the live wiki, which is a more direct, quick way of getting user feedback. If you're contemplating moving large amounts of data, then you could create the new "parent" sections on the live wiki and move just a few key pages into them. Tell people to take a look, and see what the fallout is.

You could treat it as an "agile" project: do a bit, then try it out. Iterate and improve constantly, making sure you have a plan but being ready to change the plan as you go along.

Why? Because it's a bit scary and off-putting to think of it as such a large project – both for the wiki-gardener and for the wiki consumers. Bite-sized chunks may be easier to deal with

In short, any redesign must be as carefully thought out as the original wiki implementation. Consider why you are doing the redesign and what problems you are trying to solve, then test each potential solution.

Redesign is Inevitable – Be Prepared

Redesign is an inevitable part of maintaining a wiki. The impact of redesign can be lessened and the effectiveness increased by being aware that redesign will be happen at some point.

The best way to approach this is to build in a regular design review into the wiki maintenance check list (see Chapter 6, *Maintaining the Garden*). Also make sure to allow time in the project schedule for refining design work (you do have a wiki project schedule, don't you?). That way, when a landscaping project becomes necessary it won't come as a surprise, and time and resources will already be scheduled rather than having to be found at the last minute.

8

Organic Growth

Cross-Fertilization

When one wiki becomes successful in an organization, it can help seed and speed the implementation and growth of other wiki projects. When other user communities see the benefits of using a wiki they will invariably start to see places where they too could benefit from using a wiki. You will also find that people who contribute to and use a successful wiki will begin to expect that, no matter what project they are working on, a wiki will be in place to support cross-functional collaboration and enable knowledge sharing.

The inherent cross-functional nature of wikis means that team members from one project are likely to be involved in other projects and departments and will bring their wiki experiences with them. This, "I used a wiki over there, so I expect to be able to use one over here," mind set will help propagate wikis across an organization. In these cases the secondary wikis have a greater chance of growth and success, as they are based on clear perceived need, plus those who champion them tend to have positive experiences using wikis.

Single Login

One way to encourage cross-fertilization and growth of existing wikis is to provide a single login. When people request a login for one wiki, provide them with a login that works on other associated wikis, or other corporate systems such as bug-trackers, expense report submission forms, etc. Once activated, let them know that they now have access to other wikis that might interest them and encourage them to contribute there as well.

For instance, at WebWorks.com customers requesting logins for either the Customer Projects or Documentation wikis automatically get access to both. This technique has demonstrably encouraged cross-fertilization. People who have experience using one wiki are less likely to be intimidated about contributing to another, and they tend to think, "I have access, so I may as well use it and contribute."

Cross Linking

Perhaps the greatest strength of the World Wide Web is the ability to easily embed links from one piece of information to another. In fact, it's this very behavior and the resultant cross-linking that gives the web its name. This same philosophy also applies to wikis, after all a wiki is an editable web page and therefore supports the same sort of hyperlink technology that makes cross-linking possible. In addition to using hyperlinks in your wiki to link to additional content and information on traditional websites, also use them to link to other wikis.

Including links from one wiki to another will help make the community members more aware of the other wiki (or wikis) that you wish to promote. With increased familiarity will come an increased awareness of the value they can add, and a desire and willingness to contribute to multiple wikis.

Community Gardening

In many ways developing a wiki culture is a lot like building a community garden where knowledge and knowledge sharing are the main products.

Wikis grow best through community, and there are many ways to reach current and potential community members. Most of the techniques discussed so far revolve around peer influence within a physical environment, an office, company, etc. But there are other techniques that can be used to promote wiki use and growth.

Due to their collaborative nature, wikis are often called a Web 2.0 technology. However, this is not strictly accurate, since they predate what we think of as Web 2.0 by a few years. Web 2.0 is generally used to describe the movement away from static webpages to dynamic, shareable content and the rise of social networking applications. The term Web 2.0 was first coined in 2004, ten years after the development of the first wiki.

Yet Web 2.0 tools, and social networks in particular, can be valuable assets in helping to promote and grow a wiki. The easiest and most effective technique is to build awareness of the wiki in other places that potential community members go.

This can be as simple as answering questions on an email group or making comments on blog posts that include links back to relevant articles in the wiki. Several software companies have used this technique, posting answers to questions asked on email lists with links to the relevant sections of their documentation wikis. Within a short period of time members of the email lists started both contributing to the wiki and posting wiki links themselves when answering other users questions.

Building Community

Check where your user community spends its time online, and use those destinations to promote the wiki. You could use social network tools like Twitter or Facebook, or write blog posts about the wiki and its value. Cross-pollination with social network tools can work both ways.

Many wikis provide widgets or macros that you can use to embed content from other web services onto your wiki page, such as a macro that will display live streams from Twitter, a set of photographs from Flickr, a YouTube video, and so on. You can use this sort of integration to attract people to the wiki who are already involved in other types of social media.

You can also use traditional, static websites as a way to promote your wiki through techniques like click-through buttons or banner ads. Email campaigns, mentions in company newsletters, and case studies at conferences and in industry media are also effective ways to raise awareness.

The best advocates for a wiki are invariably the community members themselves. If you make the wiki a place of real value where the community members feel that their contributions are recognized, then they will want to share and invite others.

As mentioned earlier, verbal feedback, such as a simple verbal "nice wiki article," can be a very effective way of encouraging wiki use. However such feedback tends to be limited to the individual, or a physically co-located peer group and is not necessarily visible to the community as a whole

Here are some other techniques you can use to recognize and reward contributions for a community which includes remote contributors:

Points systems

In a points system, people are given points based on types of activity. For instance one networking site I use has the following scheme:

- ► Logging in – 1 point
- ► Setting up a profile homepage – 10 points
- ► Posting a comment – 5 points
- ► Contributing an article – 20 points
- ► Editing an article – 10 points
- ► Referring a new contributor – 15 points

The concept behind this approach is to give the biggest contributors to the community the most visibility. A good points system shouldn't be designed just to help earn a better position, but to encourage people to do the things that are going to help everyone get the most value from the community

MVP programs

Once you have a way of tracking who the most active members of the community are and who contributes the most, you can recognize those contributions by developing categories of users. Many online forums already use this technique, where they apply different "ranks" as the number of posts you add increases.

Applying some sort of reward to the top "rank" users and contributors can make activity on the wiki a desirable activity with a tangible benefit. That benefit could be peer recognition or even a financial reward.

One software company I have worked with recognizes their top customer contributors each year as MVPs and in addition to the usual T-shirts and coffee mugs, gives them a free personal annual license to the software, discounts to their user conference, and early access to product releases.

Spotlight articles

Another technique to recognize contributors is to have a series of spotlight articles on the wiki homepage. These can either be articles by your MVP contributors or interesting articles by new contributors. Rotating these on a regular basis, such as once a week, keeps the front page of the wiki fresh and provides more opportunities for recognition.

Reaching Critical Mass

An argument can be made that at some point a wiki will reach a critical mass where it will become self-sustaining. For instance, consider Wikipedia: even though new information is being added and existing information edited all the time, there is really no more need to promote Wikipedia. In fact, growth in the number of people who contribute to this online encyclopedia has almost flat-lined. That is, while there may be different individual contributors over a given stretch of time, the actual overall number of contributors is fairly constant.

With most wikis the growth in the number of contributors in the early days may be slow, but as awareness increases you should expect to see a sudden upward trend. The most common case is to see a spike in contributor numbers and activity around the time of educational events, for example wiki training. However, the underlying trend through these spikes will still be one of steady growth.

After a period of time growth will slow down, especially as the wiki reaches its critical mass of information (or if it's a wiki designed to support a specific project, as the project nears completion). The growth may even flat-line, although as with Wikipedia, you may still be attracting new contributors.

However, by definition a wiki is never really finished. There is nearly always something else that can be added. Ideally, even at the "critical mass" stage, there will continue to be a slow incremental level of activity.

Keeping the activity level going requires effort. Don't ignore a wiki just because you feel it has reached critical mass. Once a wiki stops being updated, it will quickly lose its relevance and start to be ignored.

Most of the above applies to the sort of wiki that is intended to be a knowledge base or intranet. There are other types of wiki, such as those used for a specific collaborative project (e.g., editing this book) or to plan a specific event. If you don't expect the wiki to grow after a certain date, either in terms of number of contributors or in terms of new content, then you'll need to consider whether to keep the wiki online as an ongoing reference or for historical interest. This may be worth doing, even if there are no resources to "grow" it any further.

9

Harvesting the Information

User-Generated Content

One of the most appealing aspects of implementing a wiki is the prospect of getting feedback from the community that uses it. In the case of wikis based around corporate processes or products, this can mean getting contributions from people over whom you have no direct authority.

This concept of "user-generated content" is often cited as a potential roadblock to implementing a wiki, as it is felt that such "unofficial" contributions will devalue the information.

In fact the opposite is true.

As pointed in the introduction to this book, collaboration is often the key to achieving results that are greater than the sum of the efforts of individual participants. When it comes to products, the people who know the most about them are often your customers. Particularly in the world of software, although it applies to other products as well, it doesn't matter how many scenarios you design and test for, your customers will find ways to use your product that you never thought of. They use your products regularly, and they will find both faults and new uses. They are creating information that is invaluable to you and your other customers.

The concept of user-generated content is neither new nor is it solely associated with wikis. In fact, for the majority of human history this has been the normal way that information is communicated. One person comes up with an idea, a thought, or a story; and as it is repeated each teller adds his or her own contribution. The tradition of oral knowledge sharing is an ancient one that readily accepts the axiom that the community will add and embellish to the benefit of all. (See my presentation, "Why Publishing is No Longer the Last Step,"[1] for more on these ideas.)

The modern belief in the sanctity and veracity of the written word is a relatively recent product of 19th and early 20th century thinking.

[1] http://www.slideshare.net/webworks/why-publishing-is-no-longer-the-last-step-2513597

In the early days of written communication, prior to the development of the printing press, texts were copied by hand, with each scribe adding commentary and input. Even in the early days of the printing press, print runs were small and changes were often made to manuscripts and texts between printings in reaction to social and political changes.

Even Shakespeare used customer feedback, plus input from other writers, in his work. What we now consider the definitive works are in fact just snapshots of a particular version of each play. Modern scholarship shows that Shakespeare would change parts of plays, often on a daily basis, reacting to audience feedback and events of the day. In many ways his works were "The Daily Show" of Elizabethan England. Shakespeare wrote for the stage and his audience, not for the written word and posterity. He was open to ideas from his customer base, and we should be, too.

Within my two-decade career in technical and corporate communications, I have come across numerous examples of user-generated content that pre-date the wiki and web technology.

In the later years of high school, like many teenage boys, a lot of my life revolved around mending old cars. Most of my reading in those days was Haynes repair manuals. Tucked away in the back of those manuals was a postcard on which you could send in your own tips and tricks and corrections to the procedures. I don't know how many of those greasy thumb-print covered cards my friends and I sent in over the years, but I do recall our celebration the day we found one of our tips included in an updated version of one of the manuals.

One of my first jobs in the technical communication industry was writing repair documentation for the Concorde supersonic aircraft. At that point the aircraft was only operated by two airlines, British Airways and Air France, both of which had the authority to make engineering changes. As a result, it wasn't long before a British Airways Concorde differed significantly from an Air France Concorde. As we maintained and wrote the documentation for both airlines, they would submit the changes and we would put them into the manual, flagged as what we termed a COC (Customer Originated Change). Some pages would carry a British Airways masthead and others an Air France masthead. This was user-generated content, it just took time for it to be incorporated into the final product.

With wiki technology this basic idea of accommodating user-generated feedback has been made more explicit and the speed of incorporation increased to the point where it can be, but doesn't have to be, instantaneous.

The Myth of Inaccuracy

Another of the great myths about wikis is that because they can be edited by anybody they will be inaccurate.

Firstly, as we discussed earlier, "anyone" doesn't really mean "everyone." You decide who can contribute to the wiki and how they can contribute. So, you can limit access to those you trust. However, be aware that as you tighten access you may end up with just the opinions of a small number of contributors, and you won't be able to harvest the collective knowledge and experience of the community.

If you are going to lock a wiki down so tightly that only a privileged few can contribute and no one can comment, then you may as well just set up a traditional static website or even produce a printed (or PDF) version of your information. However, if you don't want anyone to contribute to your content, but you do want a mechanism for encouraging and harvesting feedback, then a tightly controlled wiki may still add value.

It may seem natural to assume that the larger the pool of contributors, the greater the opportunity for inaccuracy. Yet a 2005 study by the academic magazine, Nature, cited by Stewart Mader in *Wikipatterns*[5], showed that the most open wiki, Wikipedia, is no less accurate than the Encyclopedia Britannica, and that when mistakes do occur they are corrected much more quickly. In wikis with larger communities, people with particular areas of interest will tend to monitor and review the pages that match their own areas of expertise and fix mistakes quickly.

A wiki's roll-back capability also means that if mistakes or inaccuracies are introduced, it is very easy to restore a previous version.

Defining User-Generated Content.

When setting up your wiki you need to consider what sort of user-generated content you want. Do you want to let members of your community add new pages, edit existing pages, or just comment on pages? Or do you want to give various combinations of these privileges to different groups of users?

These decisions and privileges may differ from page to page, section to section, and user to user within a particular wiki. And, if you have multiple wikis, you may want to set different permission patterns for different communities.

Here are four basic levels of permission that you can consider:

- ► **Create New Pages:** Users can create new pages. This is a great way to discover gaps in your information model. However, you have to be aware that it is almost inevitable that you will get duplicate pages. Also note that just because someone creates a new page, or a link to a new page, it does not necessarily mean that they will create the content for that page.

- ► **Edit Existing Pages:** Users can edit or add new content to an existing page. This is one of the most valuable aspects of having a wiki, after all in many ways it is the whole purpose of the wiki. You need to consider how you will review and manage that content. (See the next section for more on this subject.)

- ► **Add comments:** Users can add separate comments to a page, but cannot edit the contents of that page. Locking users into a comment-only mode can be useful when you have "approved" content that must never be changed, such as legal disclaimers, safety notices, etc.

► **Delete Pages:** Users can delete existing pages. This privilege is something that would normally only be given to the wiki gardener or a system administrator, and it should be used with great caution. Often it is better to delete or move the content, but leave the page in place with a note explaining why the content has been moved or deleted.

Managing the New Content

In all of these cases you have to consider how you will monitor and control this user-generated information.

While it is true that there are no pre-existing rules on how you should set up and use a wiki, it is up to you and your users to develop a series of policies, procedures, and best practices that work for your wiki.

In a corporate environment, you will most likely need some sort of editorial review and approval process. Even Wikipedia has instituted review and approval processes for its more high-profile pages. You may need someone to monitor recent changes and interact with contributors. That same person may also need to be available to answer comments, make observations, etc.

In a more technical environment you may need someone who can review changes and comments for technical accuracy, relevancy, and other factors that might cause safety, liability, and warranty is-sues.

Various wikis provide different tools beyond just a recent changes list for content moderators and auditors to use. With some wikis you can set up RSS feeds and receive alerts when specific pages are altered. Some wikis provide daily email digests of activity, email alerts of changes to specific pages, or even the ability to "follow" specific users and monitor their activity.

For example, the wiki used to write this book sends email to me and my editor whenever a page is changed. That way, I can review his edits and comment quickly if I disagree with or don't understand a particular change, and he can watch my progress as I write.

Managing Content Ownership

One thing you need to consider with user-generated content is who owns that content. Do you consider the information to be in the public domain, or does the fact that the user logged in imply permission for you to reuse his or her contribution? Will you add attribution to contributions? Is the information on your wiki under something like a creative commons license?[2]

With an internal wiki, none of these is really an issue because all information added to the blog will be created under the terms of a typical work-for-hire employment contract where creative work and intellectual property developed on company time is owned by the company.

But with a public facing wiki, especially one where you are actively encouraging user-generated content and comments, you need to decide on your stance on all of these issues before you open the wiki to users.

Whatever your reuse policy is, you need to state it on the wiki homepage so that potential contributors are informed before they apply for a login. One approach is to develop a set of Contributor Guidelines, a full Disclaimer, and a User Agreement.

For instance, Atlassian, the makers of the Confluence wiki platform has a section on their documentation wiki clearly labeled "Contributing to Confluence Documentation" that outlines the steps and permissions needed before you can change or create information on the wiki.

Atlassian allows anyone to make changes to the developer document-ation (API guides, plugin development and gadget development), provided they have signed up for a wiki username and are logged in to the wiki, but for changes to the product documentation, they

---

[2] http://creativecommons.org/

ask that you first sign a Contributor License Agreement (CLA). The purpose of the agreement is to define the terms under which intellectual property has been contributed to the Atlassian Documentation Wiki, and would allow the company to defend the documentation wiki if a legal dispute arose concerning the contributed content.

Atlassian also clearly states that its documentation is published under a Creative Commons "cc-by" license. This means that anyone can copy, distribute, and adapt the documentation provided they acknowledge the source. The cc-by license is shown in the footer of every page, so that those who contribute to the documentation know that their contributions fall under the same copyright.

Before you start a wiki implementation, do some research into how people who have set up similar wikis have addressed this issue, and see if the solutions they have adopted will also work for you.

You should discuss different licensing options with your company's legal team to make sure you follow company guidelines and practices.

Incorporating Feedback

So now that you have feedback, what do you want to do with it?

Once new text or changes to existing text have been approved, it is simply a case of making the revised page the current display page.

The bigger question revolves around comments. Do you just leave them attached to the page for all time, or do you systematically review, incorporate, and delete old comments?

One practical approach is the following:

- ► Monitor all comments and post a response to each so that the person who posted the comment knows it has been read.

- ► Let people know that a comment or suggested change is being considered or has been approved for incorporation.

- For wikis that support multiple versions of a product (such as software), create a new wiki space for each version of the product. Leave comments related to a specific version with that version's text. If a comment suggests something will be used in the next version, then make a note to that effect. In the next version's wiki instance, post the original with the feedback incorporated and allow a new set of comments on that version.

Another approach is to use a "traffic light" system where each page or block of text has next to it a visual indicator or icon showing its approval status.

- New text that has yet to be approved has a "red light" icon.

- User-contributed text that is under review, or in the case of technical processes, has not been verified, has a "yellow light" icon.

- Text that has either not been changed since initial issue or contains reviewed and tested user-generated content has a "green light" icon.

This technique gives visitors a quick visual indication of the approval status of any information on the site.

Publishing to the Wiki from Other Sources

Up until this point I have mainly talked about creating and maintaining content on a wiki, only touching on the idea of the wiki as a destination for imported content during the initial population phase. However wikis can be used, and particularly in the technical documentation arena, are used as a publishing destination. This sort of workflow involves creating and maintaining your content elsewhere, usually in a dedicated authoring tool such as Microsoft Word, Adobe FrameMaker, an XML editor, or a help authoring tool, and then periodically publishing to a wiki. There are several tools available that allow you to set up a wiki as a distinct target format in a regular publishing process.

Round-Tripping

As more and more wikis are deployed to share business content, especially technical documentation, an idea that has been gaining in popularity is the concept of "round-tripping." In her book, *Conversation and Community*[4], Anne Gentle defines round-tripping as "the conversion from source to wiki and back." This generally means taking your source content, converting it to a wiki output, collecting the changes made on the wiki, and incorporating them back into the source files before starting another round of editing and publishing.

Most companies that have documentation wikis already do this as a manual process. When I hear people using the phrase "round-tripping" they tend to be talking in terms of automating the process. When I have asked people what the business case is for implementing automated round-tripping, very few have an answer beyond "well it would be cool."

One notable exception where automated round-tripping may be of benefit is with a multilingual wiki. For instance, I recently heard about a wiki with a community base of 90,000 users that had copies of the base English wiki in twenty-two other languages. To ensure a true global reach, the community had no requirement that members speak English to have access to the wiki. In this instance, round-tripping would have to be coordinated with language translation memory systems to ensure a simultaneous update. A daunting task, but one that would have a measurable impact.

If you think that you need round-tripping between your wiki and your source documents, think carefully about what you really need. Consider if there are any consequences to altering the source material. There may be legal and liability issues related to such changes. Going back to my days in aerospace documentation; in the unfortunate instance of an aircraft accident, all the work on the documentation was frozen, and we had to be able to reproduce the exact version of the documentation that was used the last time that particular aircraft was serviced. If you had automatic round-tripping of user-generated content into the source content, satisfying such a request would require your wiki management and control systems to be synchronized with your document management and content version control systems.

It might seem that the best way to approach round-tripping is to develop a scripted, automated system to incorporate feedback and changes into the source content. However, this approach is also fraught with potentially harmful consequences. Without checks and balances you may overwrite sensitive information and potentially cause liability, safety, and warranty issues.

If the end result of round-tripping is important to you, and you do not want to go through the manual process of incorporating feedback and wiki changes into the source documentation, you might consider using the wiki itself as the new source for any changes after the initial publication cycle. That is, use the wiki as your authoring environment.

If you cannot use the wiki as an authoring environment – perhaps because you need to leverage the efficiencies, knowledge, and investment in existing authoring tools, or you need to create high-quality output alongside the wiki from a single content source – then round-tripping may be an essential part of your process.

In such instances, you need to make sure that your process still includes what I term the "human element." No matter how much you manage to automate, you still need to include a person in the process who can ensure that all content coming from the wiki is appropriate, has been reviewed, and (if necessary) approved. This person also needs to ensure that the new content is correctly attributed and does not overwrite sensitive information.

Publishing from a Wiki

As groups develop wikis and build knowledge bases around them, there has been an increasing demand for tools and techniques to use information in a wiki as the source content for various types of publishing. These types of activities fall into a variety of scenarios, including the following possibilities:

- ► Using information created in a wiki by engineers and designers as source information for technical and instructional documentation.

- ► Delivering wiki content in other online deliverable formats such as online help, PDFs, or mobile device formats.

- ► Pulling together a selection of wiki pages on related topics and packaging them as a single deliverable – a practice known as wiki-slicing.

- ► Using wiki content as the single source for delivering publications in different formats, such as print and eBooks (as we did with this book).

None of these is particularly difficult to implement. As we mentioned earlier in the book, most wikis have an underlying markup language, called wiki text, that is used to denote both the structure and format of the content. While the specifics of the wiki text markup may vary from wiki to wiki, most wikis today, and certainly all of the most popular ones, include an ability to convert the content from the underlying proprietary wiki text to industry standard markup languages such as HTML (for web display) or XML (for publishing).

Once information is in a wiki, it isn't locked there; building and growing a wiki isn't the end point of a project. In many cases it can be the start of using that content in new ways that may not have been previously available.

10

A Cornucopia of Content

Now that you have decided a wiki is right for your project or organization, selected a wiki platform, planned and implemented it, and built your community, what do you do now?

Ongoing Maintenance

Like any good garden, a wiki will have a mix of annuals (content you only need to work with for a short time), perennials (content that you will work with on a regular basis), and even dormant seeds (content and ideas that have proven to be of little actual value). You will need to keep doing some pruning, landscaping, and the occasional bit of spring-cleaning to keep the content fresh and relevant.

Once your wiki is established, it will fall into one of the following categories in terms of maintenance:

Archival

A wiki built for a single purpose, with a specific goal in mind. These project-oriented wikis may not be needed once a project is complete and the specific goal achieved. However, it may be useful to maintain them for archival purposes. This may mean removing editing permission for all except the wiki gardener, while still giving community members permission to read and comment.

Periodic

A wiki that is subject to regular, planned updates. A typical application might be a wiki for documentation or one related to a regular event, such as a conference. This type of wiki may lie dormant for extended periods between updates, and usage will invariably drop off as little or no new content is added.

One way to reinvigorate such a wiki and maintain interest is to hold events such as a wiki-sprint, where a team of people get together in a collaborative environment – preferably in the same physical space, such as a conference room – to create the new content in a short period of time. This jump starts content updates, shows the community that the wiki is active, and encourages others to contribute new content.

Continuous

A knowledge-base wiki where you expect ongoing, unplanned contributions. The primary ongoing task with a wiki of this type is continuing to promote awareness. You need to continually demonstrate the value of the wiki as a resource and a collaborative tool. Inviting new users into the community – for example by having new employees set up their own home page – is an excellent way to keep interest levels high and promote new contributions. Using some of the feedback and reward methods mentioned earlier can also help retain interest.

Of course the best incentive for people to keep using a wiki of any type is to make sure that it has content that provides real value and that it continues to give participants a sense of belonging to a community that respects and uses their work.

So What About the "Fun & Profit"?

The title of this book is *WIKI: Grow Your Own for Fun & Profit.* So what about the fun and profit? Over the preceding chapters I hope that I have helped explain the many ways that a wiki can be used to the benefit of companies, individuals, and above all communities with a shared interest or goal.

Being part of a community that delivers tangible benefits and opens up lines of communication can be a fun experience. In general, I have found that once you get involved in knowledge sharing, it becomes an activity that you look forward to, and that enables you to develop a wider appreciation for what others do. As a friend of mine recently observed, "technically, it's not the collaborative technology that rocks. It's the people using it who rock."

I asked several wiki users what aspects of using a wiki they considered to be fun. Here's a sample of their responses:

- ► Being part of a team / community
- ► Sharing your knowledge
- ► Helping solve problems
- ► Learning new stuff

- Learning about your colleagues
- Finding out what happens in other parts of the organization
- Knowing where you fit in the big picture
- Feeling that what you have to offer has value

The word profit in the book's title doesn't relate to monetizing the wiki itself (although in certain circumstances that might be an option), but is more an indication of how the various efficiencies and changes in procedure and behavior discussed in the earlier chapters can have a positive impact on an organization's bottom line.

For instance, increased efficiencies can result in significant cost savings:

- Less email traffic means less productive time lost to your inbox
- Wiki collaboration means fewer meetings and less time lost
- Fewer meetings can reduce travel costs
- With project or company information located in one central resource, less time is lost locating information
- Less information is "lost," so less time and money are spent recreating lost information
- Greater visibility across your organization can reduce duplication of effort

Companies that use wikis to share information and connect with their customers can see significant reductions in support costs.[1]

This is primarily due to two factors:

- Information is easier to find
- Customers become self-sufficient

Improved communication with customers, especially in a community environment, can generate opportunities to increase revenue. According to LaSandra Brill, Senior Manager, Social Media Marketing, Cisco Systems, during 2009, companies that engaged in community-

---

[1]In my personal experience, I have seen as much as a 50% reduction.

driven conversations with their customers saw revenues increase by just under 20%. (Cisco and the Social Web[2])

A Final Stroll Around the Garden

I hope that the previous pages will prove to be a guide that helps you implement your wiki project. If I have one central theme that I'd like you to come away with, it's that wiki implementation is not about the technology, it's as much an exercise in sociology as anything else.

Managing change and learning to apply new behavior patterns is as crucial, if not more so, than selecting which wiki platform you will use. While changes in social computing, such as blogs and social network sites, have shown that it is OK to comment on someone else's work, thoughts, and ideas; the concept of changing the written word can still be daunting for some people.

The key is that while the word *WIKI* is in the title of this book and is the technology we've been discussing, what we are really talking about is *collaboration.*

If you have knowledge, then share it. The community will benefit.

---

[2] http://www.marketingprofs.com/marketing/online-seminars/275/

Case Study 1

A Wiki-Driven Company

Company:	WebWorks.com
Location:	Austin, Texas, USA
Purpose:	Multiple wikis to support different parts of the business

WebWorks.com,[1] an Austin, Texas-based division of Quadralay Corporation, is the developer of the ePublisher platform, a product that allows users to take information created in nearly any format, then convert and publish that content to a wide range of digital delivery formats, including, MediaWiki, MoinMoin, and Confluence.

WebWorks.com considers itself a "wiki-driven company," not because it produces wiki software, but because wikis have become an integral part of the way the company operates and conducts business with its customers. At the time of writing, the company had five active wikis, three of them open to the public, one shared with select customers, and one that is purely internal.

The company installed its first wiki in 2003 as a way for the software development team to share information and collaborate across different design and development disciplines. Based on the success of the development team wiki, in 2005 the company's Services Group selected the Project Trac solution, with its built-in wiki, as a way to enable collaboration and improve communication with select customers, who were often located in different time zones and countries.

---

[1] http://WebWorks.com

In 2007, the company standardized on the MoinMoin wiki platform and the development wiki was expanded to become a company wide "inner wiki" replacing the static HTML intranet. Later that year the company launched its first external wiki, a "Help Center"[2] wiki where customers could exchange information with the support and development teams, as well as help each other out on projects or post general usage tips and tricks.

The next website to make the move to a wiki was the one used to promote and organize the company's annual users conference. In 2008, WebWorksRoundup.com made the transition from a traditional HTML-based website to a wiki. This made it quick and easy both for conference organizers to update the site and for speakers to add biographical information and presentation abstracts without editorial or process bottlenecks.

In 2009, the company made good on a promise delivered at the previous year's user conference and published all their product documentation online in a public wiki (http://docs.webworks.com), allowing the user community to provide feedback and comments and giving the company a way to quickly test and incorporate suggestions in subsequent releases. At the time of writing, the documentation wiki includes information covering all supported versions of their products.

The WebWorks Wikis

Inner wiki

The company's "inner wiki" is now used for every aspect of company business, and a cultural paradigm of "if it isn't on the wiki, it doesn't exist" has developed. In other words, the wiki has become the depository of record.

There was a surprisingly short learning curve for the wiki, with the initial staff training taking less than an hour. Subsequent updates, such as communicating changes from an upgrade, have usually been

---

[2] http://wiki.webworks.com

accomplished during a brown-bag lunch session. Using the inner wiki has drastically reduced the amount of time needed to bring new employees up to speed. Introducing new employees to the wiki established and cemented a company culture of open information flow and collaboration that helped reduce duplication of effort, brought down operational costs, and shortened sales cycles.

A survey of wiki usage undertaken in early 2009 revealed that 90% of the company employees had made at least one contribution to the inner wiki, 80% contributed about once a month, and 50% contributed once a week. These usage figures are exceptionally high and are a reflection of a small, technology-focused company whose core business is based on information exchange.

Another significant factor in driving such high usage rates is that the company's senior management is fully committed to the use of wikis. They review contributions each day, provide regular feedback, and are among the top contributors. The open structure of the wiki also promotes cross-functional collaboration and information sharing.

Help Center wiki

The Help Center wiki was set up to promote information exchange with, and between, customers. As such it is an open, public wiki. The wiki was initially populated with articles written by WebWorks development and support engineers. Once the wiki was launched these groups have continued to add new content regularly.

One of the first lessons learned in setting up an open wiki was dealing with spam. It became quickly apparent that the wiki manager would need to set up a user login request and approval system. Today a user's request is usually checked and approved in less than two hours.

It took a while for customers to start contributing, but persistence paid off. The initial indication that customers were using the wiki was when they started to reference, and provide links to, wiki articles in the independent users group mailing list. Gradually they started to request login approval. Growth is now steady, and at the time of writing there is usually at least one request a day. Customer contributions average about one a week. It also became clear that the wiki benefited from the development of "cheer leaders," who saw the benefits of participation early and advocated using the wiki to the user community.

Another area that caused some initial concern was how to differentiate between what was official company information and what wasn't. Various flagging schemes were discussed, and the company decided that the simplest solution would be to lock permissions on pages of official information so customers could only post comments, but leave discussions and un-tested information open to both editing and comments.

Conference wiki

Moving the conference information from a static website to a wiki, then opening the wiki to conference organizers and giving restricted access to speakers, removed several bottlenecks and helped ensure that the website was kept up-to-date at all times. However, there were aspects of using the wiki that caused some small problems. It was harder to give the wiki-driven site the correct corporate look and feel; while it was easy to update text, graphics handling was not as sophisticated as an HTML-based site. In order to make it look more like a traditional website, WebWorks decided to turn off the visible wiki edit controls. This meant that contributors needed to take extra steps to login and make edits.

Services wiki

The services wiki was implemented to facilitate communications and knowledge sharing with customers during customer-driven custom development projects. The primary aim was to eliminate problems associated with multiple, parallel, and branching email trails. The wiki was designated as the single point of contact and official source of information on project status. Any communication outside the wiki was deemed to be unofficial. At the start of each project a one hour online web conference was held to establish guidelines and teach the customer how to use the wiki.

Information such as the project description, list of deliverables, contacts, notes, reference materials, and a deliverable log were uploaded to the wiki and could be updated by any member of the project team.

Even with training it took some customers a while to change their behavior and switch from sending project information in email. Some time was invested in transcribing customer email onto the wiki to demonstrate the advantages of having information in a single repository. However, once customers made the adjustments and everyone started working from the same data set, there were measurable decreases in the time taken to deliver tasks and resolve issues. Projects were delivered quicker, with little or no scope creep, and at less cost.

Documentation wiki

The rollout of the WebWorks documentation wiki was the culmination of a six-month project to rewrite the main product documentation set and use the company's own product to publish it. The content was written using Structured FrameMaker and then used as a single source in conjunction with WebWorks ePublisher to simultaneously produce PDF, embedded online help, and wiki output.

The project was managed using the services wiki, with a phased release to test and review the wiki portion. As a first phase, invitations to the new wiki were restricted to recognized MVP-level users for review. After the input of these highly knowledgeable users, the wiki was opened up to anyone with a current active support account. Then, at the conclusion of further testing, it was opened up to the public at large. Now anyone who is approved for a login to the documentation wiki also gets automatic access to the Help Center wiki, and vice versa.

With each new release of the product, a snapshot of the latest state of the document wiki for the previous software version is taken and placed in its own section on the wiki. There are now separate wiki spaces with documentation for each supported version of the product.

A recent innovation has been linking the online help embedded in the product with the public documentation wiki. If the WebWorks ePublisher platform is installed on a computer with Internet access, then when a user opens an online help topic, the help system will check the corresponding topic on the wiki and flag the topic if the content has been updated on the wiki since product release or if there has been active discussion on that topic on the wiki.

Without the extensive use of wiki technology in all areas of its operations, WebWorks would not be able to work as efficiently as it does in supporting its partners and customers worldwide. Cross-functional collaboration, combined with knowledge sharing and listening to customers, is central to the company's continued growth.

Case Study 2

Building an International Community

Company:	Outward Bound
Location:	Sandy, Utah, USA
Purpose:	Consolidating information from disparate international group

> *There is more in us, the collective us, than we know, and*
> *if we can be made to see it, we'll never settle for less.*
> —Kurt Hahn, founder of Outward Bound

Outward Bound International's (OBI)[1] mission is to help people discover and develop their potential to care for themselves, others, and the world around them through challenging experiences in unfamiliar settings.

At the time of writing there are Outward Bound schools located in 34 different countries offering a variety of courses that are aligned with its operating principles of character development, adventure and challenge, learning through experience, compassion and service, and social and environmental responsibility.

While the details of the courses may vary from location to location, the core principles and many of the operating procedures are common. However, not all the different international organizations were in sync, and due to geographical distance, OBI found that rather

---

[1] http://outward-bound.org

than building on experience and knowledge of older, more established, locations, there was a high duplication of effort in establishing new schools.

The result of these findings was the creation of the Outward Bound International World Resources Project. The project's three main strategic goals were the following:

1. Serve as a useful central resource

2. Empower an international network

3. Coordinate network & resources

To support these strategic goals, the project team developed a further set of operational and technical goals, including the following:

- Collect online resources & encourage contributions

- Grow vibrant international network of staff and affiliates

- Provide online professional development opportunities

- Provide online access to equipment discounts

- Encourage international network collaboration using social software tools

- Provide updated method for storing/sharing resources (wiki)

- Provide online vehicles for collaboration (wiki / social media / Web2.0 tools)

- Provide training in use of collaborative web tools

- Assess usefulness of tools and strength of network

After the wiki had been selected and sample content added, the first test of the project was to train Outward Bound staff members on the use and capabilities of the new platform. To do this Outward Bound set up a series of "wikifest" training sessions. These were a mix of in-person workshops (held at seven different global locations) and online webinars in order to reach the largest possible number of potential contributors.

After the first 12 months of operation, the Outward Bound International wiki had attracted 2,029 users and contained 8,287 pages of information. Total page views numbered over 176,000, with just over 34,000 page edits. While the number of wiki page views per month varied – for example, there were noticeable spikes in activity around the time of scheduled training sessions – the underlying trend was positive, growing from 5,000 page views per month to 20,000 page views per month over a 12 month period.

There was also a noticeable increase in activity per user as community members became more familiar with the content and as the value of the content increased. One technique used to introduce the wiki, and to get community members comfortable in contributing and editing content, was to ask each person to complete an online profile (branded as the WikiHR Database), which, in addition to collecting basic information, offered members the chance to share information on subjects and activities that interested them.

Through their own participation, senior management encourages use of the wiki as a way to share knowledge and increase communication between regional centers of operation. Each month a wiki newsletter publishes the latest usage statistics, highlighting new content and specific areas of interest.

The wiki is now so central to Outward Bound operations that knowledge management is built into each Outward Bound school's annual business plan, and each school has appointed a person to act as "Knowledge Management Liaison."

Thanks to the shared knowledge aspect of the wiki, a set of best practices has been developed that allows new Outward Bound schools to build on the experiences of other schools. The result is a more efficient set-up process, which has led to new schools being fully operational more quickly than before. Operationally, Outward Bound has moved from separate national islands of information acting under the same brand name to a true international community.

Outward Bound International is now building on its wiki implementation knowledge and experience by developing sister wiki sites for some of its affiliate brands. As well as providing internal operational benefits, the wiki has enabled Outward Bound to position itself as an industry shaper as well as a product leader, enabling it to make a much greater impact at a strategic level.

Case Study 3

Meeting a Specific Business Need

Company:	Geometrica
Location:	Houston, Texas, USA
Purpose:	Develop ISO 9000 Quality Manuals

This case study examines a wiki implementation that was built to meet a specific business need, and in doing so provided a focus for a company-wide collaboration project.

Houston, Texas-based Geometrica[1] engineers, manufacturers, and builds dome-shaped and space-frame style structures around the world. Although the company was confident of its quality control procedures, its clients were increasingly insistent on ISO 9001 certification. The company's policies and procedures were already documented in various electronic and hard copy formats, but these documents had been developed on an ad-hoc basis in response to problems, client demands, and training needs. There was no single approach or cohesive structure.

Having identified the business need to obtain the ISO 9001 certification, the company's first response was to set up a committee to write a traditional quality manual. As the committee emailed back and forth word-processed drafts, edits, comments, discussions, agreements, disagreements, meeting minutes, etc., it became apparent that the procedure was "horrendously inefficient." The process

---
[1] http://www.geometrica.com/

itself became a big part of the problem: conflicts about documents, typos, clarifications, and the organization of the information required substantial editing, even for documents that had been considered complete.

In short, their efforts to create a quality management system were disappearing in the email inbox. At this point the company started looking at wikis.

The main aim of the wiki project was to develop a system centered on the organization as a whole, not around a single person or department. The whole organization would provide feedback and shape the documentation so the end product reflected what the organization needed, not what one individual or department believed was best.

After investigating various wiki platforms, the Geometrica team selected the ProjectForum[2] wiki – a wiki specifically designed for small to medium-sized collaboration teams – based on ease of installation, maintenance, and usability.

As with many implementations, the wiki team initially faced resistance and skepticism based on worries about vandalism, poor editing, and lack of control. Other objections came from ingrained perceptions about the necessity for a sequential author, edit, approve, and publish process and the perception that when a document is published its information is generally believed to be correct, complete, permanent, and authoritative.

Once people started to use the wiki to achieve a common goal, these objections quickly disappeared. The whole company was empowered to edit any document. The distinction between author and editor disappeared as changes to documents appeared immediately in all company locations and job sites. The quality of the information improved and continues to improve. Geometrica CEO Francisco Castano cites the following reasons for the wiki's quick acceptance:

---

[2] http://www.projectforum.com/pf/

- Ease of access means that users check the wiki frequently to learn more or to verify their knowledge.

- More people get involved with much less effort. A wiki allows non-core people to pay attention to just the bits they care about.

- Ease of editing simplifies minor corrections and improvements that might otherwise be ignored because the errors were tolerable. The people who know a topic detect shortcomings and correct them immediately.

- The aggregation of many small corrections and improvements results in significant changes, otherwise known as "wiki magic."

- Information isn't repeated. The ability to include and link to other wiki pages allows information to be maintained in a single location. (This requires careful oversight because there is no built-in mechanism to avoid repetition of information).

- One rule: No rules. Because the organization is working toward one goal, anyone can share ideas, discuss, comment, change, edit, copy, and paste as needed. Everyone's skills and knowledge are welcome.

- Having managers from different areas working together on wiki documentation created a multidisciplinary approach that enhanced learning and interaction throughout the organization.

Even with such wide acceptance, the Geometrica team also acknowledged that not everyone was comfortable editing on a wiki, and given the geographic diversity of staff working on various construction projects, some people didn't have access to computers.

In those cases, Geometrica decided to let these individuals use a bug tracking database, normally designed for tracking software development bugs, to report "bugs" (i.e., errors) in the documentation. These bug reports were automatically assigned to the department heads, who moderated discussions as required and were responsible for implementing any required corrections in the wiki.

Within less than one year, the wiki had amassed 1,577 pages of high quality documentation containing more than 3 GB of data. A survey conducted at the end of 2009 revealed that each wiki page had been edited an average of 12 times, with 12 pages receiving over 100 edits. 36 people out of a staff of 100 contributed to the wiki, with the average user contributing more than 400 edits.

The main focus of the project was to assist the company in gaining ISO 9000 compliance. According to the ISO 9000 Council website, creating and writing an ISO 9000 compliant quality manual from scratch can take up to two years. Using a wiki, Geometrica completed the project in nine months. Once in place, the wiki helped Geometrica meet several different criteria in the ISO 9000 standard including the following:

► Documentation of the quality system
► Document control and management
► Record control
► Communicating statutory requirements to the organization
► Communicating policy changes
► Maintaining QMS integrity
► Defining roles and responsibilities
► Trackable internal communication process
► Management reviews
► Employee performance reviews
► Managing the design development process
► Controlling production by tracking and registering work instructions
► Internal audits
► Promoting continuous improvement

The wiki continues to be an information source for Geometrica and is central to the company's philosophy of continuous improvement.

[This case study is based in part on notes from "Using a Wiki to Implement a Quality Management System"[13] by Francisco Castano, Gerardo Mendez, Julio Ayala and Linda Day, which appeared in Quality Digest Daily, October 2009. Extracts from that article are used here with permission.]

Case Study 4

Wiki Document Content Strategy

Company:	Numara Software
Location:	Tampa, Florida, USA
Purpose:	Engaging users in document content strategy

The technical writing team at Numara Software[1] was looking for a way to gather feedback from customers on their product documentation. Neither of the two existing platforms they used to publish online help provided any facility for customers to provide comments or feedback on the quality, accuracy, or usefulness of the documentation.

Numara's own software products did include some feedback and survey capabilities, but they were not linked directly to the documentation. The feedback loop was handled by the support department, and the documentation team had no direct contact with customers. The few comments they did receive via this method were vague and difficult to link with specific documentation subjects.

The team undertook a study of feedback and customer collaboration practices in order to develop a solution that would not only have a feedback facility, but would also provide a mechanism for customers to contribute directly to the documentation itself.

---

[1] http://www.numarasoftware.com/

The existing documentation was structured to answer basic "how do I?" questions by providing detailed information on the product itself, and the support knowledge base was structured for trouble-shooting. However, there was no process for capturing specific customer use cases that could answer "how do I get the software to do this?" questions.

This sort of information is best supplied by the user community itself, since they have the most experience using the software in real-world situations. The user community had developed its own mechanisms for answering, and sharing, these sorts of questions using online forums, user group mailing lists, etc., but there was no systematic way of capturing this information and incorporating it back into the documentation.

The vision for the project was to provide a company and customer driven knowledge base, with the aim of making users self-sufficient.

Additional specific goals included the following:

- Make it easy to find information to optimize the use of Numara products
- Make it easy for the company and customers to collaborate and exchange information and knowledge.
- Present knowledge effectively for all types of users.

The project team conducted focus groups and surveyed customers on potential feedback and collaboration solutions. They found that 100% of all customers surveyed expressed a desire to contribute using a wiki. In particular, customers wanted a structured wiki with links to support and user forums, all monitored by the company.

The project team thought that using a wiki as a knowledge-base portal that included other areas of company-created content would be a good way to maintain control of the brand. Numara did not want customers searching the web for answers when a Numara wiki could give customers the most up-to-date information possible.

They felt that giving customers an organized site on which to share information would lead to the the generation of examples, best practices, lessons learned, case studies, and testimonials, and would also encourage the emergence of community leaders.

The project team wrote a product requirements document to help detail objectives, scope, constraints, resources, milestones, and stakeholders. The WikiMatrix Features List was used to develop a list of business and functional requirements, including the following:

- Cost
- Hosting
- Ability to convert content from legacy systems
- Rich text editor (WYSIWYG)
- Page history
- Security/Permissions for groups, spaces, and pages
- Navigation (table of contents with page ordering, breadcrumbs, index, etc.)
- Full-text search
- User feedback (comments)
- Notifications (email, RSS)
- Customization
- Print output (PDF)
- User forums, blogs, and personal spaces
- Statistics
- UI in English, French, German, Portuguese, and Spanish and supports translation/localization

After researching and testing several wikis, the project team settled on the Confluence wiki as best meeting their needs. The wiki was populated with a combination of legacy information imported from Microsoft Word source documents and pages written from scratch – the latter so the project leads could become familiar with the process and with the Confluence mark-up, macros, and plug-ins.

After a month of internal testing and trials, a pilot project, called the "Numara FootPrints User Community," was rolled out to customers who had participated in the focus groups. The rollout was accompanied by a newsletter promoting "The 10 Things You Can Do" as a member of the user community:

1. Share knowledge and best practices with other users and the Numara team in the FootPrints User Community space

2. Create your own wiki pages

3. Participate in the user forum

4. Create personal blog posts

5. Become a community leader

6. Provide immediate feedback with comments and questions in the help documentation pages

7. Receive notifications of recently updated pages via your personal dashboard, email notifications and/or RSS feeds)

8. View a document's page history (what changed, when, and by whom)

9. Build your own documents: export pages as Word documents or PDFs

10. Search all content at once (forum, blogs, help documentation)

As part of the pilot the team also developed a set of Contributor Guidelines, a full Disclaimer, and a User Agreement. A self-guided tutorial was also provided, and a couple of live online training sessions were offered.

The pilot project ran from April through August, 2010, during which time the team monitored the wiki for functionality, usage, feedback, and usability.

Some of the early keys to success included the following:

- ► Customer feedback that the wiki gave them what they wanted

- ► Innovative and supportive management

- ► Investment in time, research, and resources enabled positive results

- ► Open-minded content developers who were willing to give up some control over their domain in exchange for reaping the benefits of community knowledge

- ► Documenting how to use the wiki as it was developed helped develop tools to speed up user acceptance and participation

- ► Developer participation in linking the wiki to other product information sources

- ► Treating the wiki implementation as a project, with planning, schedules, etc.

- ► Using a full-featured, rich wiki that is fun for the users to interact with

- ► Taking full advantage of the wiki platform's own user community, and developing relationships with mentors and thought leaders who have used wikis in their industry

Overall, the project team found that just by using the wiki instead of working in independent "content silos" and separate help authoring systems, they improved team collaboration, communication, and productivity. They also noticed a reduction in the need to send email and spend time on the telephone. All are now literally "working off the same page."

Case Study 5

A Wiki Workflow for Publishing

Company:	XML Press
Location:	Fort Collins, Colorado, USA
Purpose:	Build high quality publications efficiently

XML Press,[1] the publisher of this book, is a small publishing company dedicated to publications for technical communicators, engineers, managers, and marketers.

When XML Press began work on *WIKI: Grow Your Own for Fun and Profit*, they wanted to take advantage of wiki technology to the greatest extent possible. They saw that wikis could help streamline their processes and increase the interaction among the author, editors, artists, and reviewers.

In addition, they wanted to experiment with new ways of authoring. Most of the books in their current and planned catalog are authored in XML, either DocBook or DITA, and their backend production processes are optimized for XML. However, not all authors are familiar with XML, and the learning curve is steep. Creating an authoring process that avoided direct authoring in XML, and provided the other benefits of a wiki, seemed like a worthy objective.

Based on advice from the author, XML Press chose PBworks, and used the hosted version (http://pbworks.com). PBworks gives authors a rich text editor, as well as the ability to directly use HTML. It ex-

---

[1] http://xmlpress.net

ports content in reasonably clean HTML, so conversion to DocBook XML was straightforward process.

Here is an outline of the development process:

- ► The author created a wiki page for the outline and separate wiki pages for each chapter, case study, and appendix, along with separate wiki pages for the preface, foreword, bibliography, and colophon.

- ► The author wrote sections in the wiki using a brief set of guidelines created by XML Press. Those guidelines described how to markup links (internal and external), footnotes, index entries, and so forth.

- ► As draft sections were completed, the primary XML Press editor reviewed them and made comments directly in the source.

- ► Periodically, the content was exported and converted to DocBook XML. Then, PDF and ePub versions of the book were generated using an automated process, and the results were then uploaded back to the wiki for review by the author.

- ► Technical review was done in the wiki, with reviewers inserting comments directly into the text. The author could then make the requested changes directly in the content.

- ► Copy-editing was done in the wiki, after which, the content was exported to DocBook XML for final production.

Overall, the only work not done in the wiki was final production of the printed and ebook versions.

Using this process had several important benefits:

- ► Until galley's needed to be reviewed for print formatting, there was no need to pass printed or PDF copies of the content between the author and editor.

- ► High levels of participation from the review team; much more than XML Press has seen with other books.

- High quality PDFs of the book-in-progress were readily available, even in the early stages of development.

- Significantly reduced production time. From the final, copy-edited version to the first printed copies was three weeks, a good part of which was spent waiting for the printer.

Appendix A

10 Questions: A Checklist

Although much of the content covered here is also included in Chapter 3: *Planting The Seed – Think Before You Implement*, I thought it would be useful to include it as a separate section that can be used as a checklist by those about to embark on a wiki project.

When I'm invited to speak to various groups about wiki implementation, I often use these 10 questions as the core of my presentation, and I have found that considering these questions before you start enables you to lay a solid foundation on which to build and grow a wiki.

I hope that you will find this summary useful as both a checklist and as a starting point for your own endeavors.

Ask yourself and your team the following questions before you start to implement a wiki, and be truthful with the answers.

Think about the issue you are trying to solve, and then see how a wiki might be applied, but remember don't just focus on the positive, think about the potential down sides too.

1. What Business Issue Will the Wiki Resolve?

For any technology implementation to succeed, there needs to be a problem to be solved, or an operational efficiency to be gained:

- ► Why you are considering a wiki?
- ► Do you have examples of wikis that address similar issues?
- ► Did they work?
- ► If so, why?

2. How Will You Measure Success?

There are two ways you could measure success. One is by setting goals for the adoption of the wiki itself. For example:

- ► What percentage of the community is contributing?
- ► How many people are registered?
- ► What is the number of new articles, or the number and frequency of comments?

The other way is to measure the wiki's success based on its impact on your business needs. For example:

- ► Did the wiki reduce the time taken for a particular process?
- ► If the wiki is a customer-facing one, how many people visited certain wiki pages?
- ► Did the wiki reduce email traffic or the number of meetings?

3. What is the Expected Return on Investment?

The first questions you will be asked about any new system will be financial:

- ► What is the financial return on investment?
- ► What are the software costs?
- ► What is the cost of populating the wiki?
- ► What is the cost of maintaining the wiki?
- ► What is the cost of training the users?
- ► What does it cost you to handle the same business functions today?

- ▸ What much do the business issues you are trying to solve affect the bottom line?
- ▸ Can you calculate the potential benefits of using a wiki? Remember that the ROI may not be directly attributable to the wiki itself, but instead may come from a change in collaboration methodologies and operational improvements.

4. Where Will the Content Come From?

Meaningful content is the key to any successful wiki, so you need to think about where it will come from. While you may be looking for the community to contribute, you will most likely need to seed the wiki:

- ▸ Where will the initial content come from?
- ▸ Will you need to invest time in creating new content, or will you import existing legacy content, such as technical documentation, training, policies and procedures, or marketing materials?
- ▸ Will you need to integrate the wiki with an existing content management system?

5. Who Will Use the Wiki Initially?

While you may be implementing a wiki to meet one particular business need, think about every area of the company, or community, that could benefit or contribute to solving that problem. Try to move beyond functional boundaries and think about the skill sets and the knowledge base of all who would benefit. In some cases this may even be people located outside the organization.

6. Who Will Use the Wiki in the Future?

Of course, one of the great things about wikis, and the central theme of this book, is that they foster growth and further collaboration. There are numerous examples of cross-pollination of wikis inside organizations as one team sees the benefits that another has gained.

Before you start your first wiki, spend some time thinking about areas of potential growth and possible future cross-functional collaboration. Make sure you make plans for scalable growth and allow easy access for anyone who may need to contribute or observe, not just on the initial projects, but on potential future ones as well.

7. Who Will Own the Wiki?

Every wiki needs an owner:

- ► Who will be your wiki-gardener?
- ► Who can you count on to be champions?
- ► Are you prepared to give up ownership – even if the idea was originally yours – in order to ensure implementation?
- ► What, if anything, will you need to do to "brand" your wiki?

8. Where Will the Wiki be Hosted?

The location and hosting of a wiki can be a contentious issue and it is one that needs addressing early:

- ► Will your IT group want to host it?
- ► Or, will they actively be against the idea?
- ► Can you host the wiki at a departmental or project team level?
- ► Should you use a third-party hosting company?
- ► If you have to, can you "fly under the radar" and avoid potentially nay-saying IT groups?

9. Which Wiki Should I Use?

There are many different types of wiki in the marketplace. Don't just decide to use one type because it's the only one you've heard of:

- ► Research your options using WikiMatrix or a similar tool.
- ► Talk to people who have used wikis for similar business needs and ask them what they used and why.
- ► Ask them which wikis they rejected and why.
- ► Look at the case studies in this book for similar situations.
- ► Develop a short list of at least three wikis to prototype and test.

10. What Controls Will I Need?

Arguably, the first rule of wikis is that there aren't any rules. It is true that wikis function best when they are driven by the communities that use them, but you need to think about a few basics of control before you start:

- ► Do you need logins, and if so who will authorize them?
- ► Will you need to hook the wiki up to an existing user base, such as Active Directory or another LDAP store, or will it be good enough to manage the users and groups entirely within the wiki?
- ► Will you have some sort of initial structure for your wiki content?
- ► Will you give users a "sandbox" area to learn the wiki in?
- ► Who will be able to see, read, and edit which pages?
- ► Who will monitor recent changes and do any necessary roll backs?
- ► What's the philosophy for rolling back content and incorporating comments?

Appendix B

Common Barriers to Adoption

During the research phase for this book, I did a straw poll among friends and business colleagues, and asked them what are the most frequent barrier statements they encounter. It quickly became clear that most of the excuses they, and I, hear for not implementing a wiki come from misconceptions and prejudices about wikis rather than actual shortfalls in the wiki technology.

It also became evident that the barriers fall into two distinct categories: cultural and technical.

Cultural Barriers

Some cultural barriers are based on assumptions and hearsay that originated in media reports about Wikipedia; others are rooted in bad experiences caused by a rush to implement. Often such barriers will inform later decisions, even though it only takes a little research to address and eliminate most cultural concerns.

Here are some of the most common "BUT" statements I hear in this category:

We tried one once and no one used it

There is a general perception that because wikis can be edited by everyone, that for a wiki to be successful everyone should contribute. Numerous studies show that no matter the technology, any collaborative project or social group will be the product of a small vocal minority. In the case of wikis, it appears that a 90-9-1 rule applies, where 90% of the user community will access the wiki just to find and read information, 9% will contribute something, but only 1% will be active contributors.

For corporate wikis with a clearly defined business purpose, the number of occasional contributors may rise to 30%, and active participants may rise to around 10% of the community. When setting up a wiki, define what an acceptable, but realistic, level of usage is and over what time scale. It can take time to build a community, and getting people to contribute needs encouragement. As with all other cultural barriers, the potential user/contributor has to see a perceived benefit from the activity.

The cost/benefit ratio is too high

One common statement I hear when discussing wikis in a business environment is the view that, "the application of a wiki does not offer enough benefit to justify the cost of maintaining it." I've heard this same sentiment voiced several times in different ways. Yes, to be successful a wiki does need maintenance – it needs someone with a sense of ownership who will do various administration tasks, such as cleaning up content and installing software updates.

But this is true of any software application. In fact, it's true of nearly all sources of information in business, from the most complex database system to the humblest of spreadsheets. To remain relevant, an information source has to be maintained. If you're going to judge any information system on its benefits, then you need to clearly define how those benefits are to be measured and what makes an acceptable return.

In the case of an information and collaboration system like a wiki, such measurements may not be as straightforward as a financial return on investment, because they may have more of a subjective social impact. But even so, a desired outcome needs to be articulated, and you need to be realistic.

I'm too busy doing actual work to try anything new

A statement like this is not just about wikis; rather, it's an indication of a fear of change – any change. The biggest challenge here is not a technical one, it's one of managing change and educating the potential audience about how the new technology or process can make their day-to-day job easier.

It's overwhelming, and I don't know where to start

This is invariably an indication that a new piece of technology, which may or may not be a wiki, has been introduced and its use was mandated without training or with no clear introductory project or need defined. Technology for technology's sake is doomed to failure.

The problem is often made worse when it is introduced by excited and enthusiastic technology geeks who overwhelm potential users with techno-babble and a "look at all the cool things this can do" attitude. With any new technology, you must first define a clear need and then map out a slow, step-by-step introductory process where benefits to the user community are clearly articulated. Start small, build familiarity, and growth will follow.

If my management doesn't care, why should I?

A very good question, and once again one that applies to new technology in general rather than wikis in particular. As with any technology, if you can clearly demonstrate the things that appeal to management / business owners, such as a measurable benefit, lower costs, and improved efficiencies, then you will start to get their attention.

One of the most interesting observations of the recent growth in the adoption of wikis is that they demonstrate this exact process. The majority of wiki implementations start with small teams, and once others begin to see the benefits, adoption spreads across the company; only then does management buy in.

It's also worth mentioning that in the opposite scenario, where a management team instigates the implementation of a wiki, the management team should be active participants. Mandating any technology and then not using it yourself is a clear indication that you have no real personal investment in it.

It won't be accurate

One of the most common and oft-repeated misconceptions of any collaborative authoring process in general, and wikis in particular, is that if a large group of people are contributing, then the influence of subject matter experts will be diluted and the resulting content will be full of inaccuracies. As noted previously, even an open, collaborative system will only attract a statistically small number of contributors. Those contributors tend to be the subject matter experts and people who have a vested interest in the subject matter. And when inaccuracies do occur, they are corrected a lot quicker than in traditional media. The net result of collaborative authoring is not only the perceived knowledge of designated experts, but also the informed contribution of others who are passionate about a subject and can bring a fresh perspective.

I prefer meetings

The best collaborative environment is the face-to-face meeting, because we communicate not only with words, but with tone, inflection, and body language. But, face-to-face meetings are not always practical, especially for a distributed team. In such instances, a collaborative workspace of any kind can be a real benefit.

Even for co-located teams, a collaborative workspace where meeting preparation and briefing documents can be compiled, reviewed, and commented on before a physical meeting can make the face-to-face sessions more efficient and productive, as participants should arrive fully briefed and aware of other participants' viewpoints.

A wiki can also be the place where the results of a meeting are communicated to non-participants and where action items can be recorded and tracked.

Technical Barriers

Technical barriers are usually the result of misconceptions about the way that wikis work or are based on reports about early versions of the technology that no longer apply. In some cases, this is analogous to saying you wouldn't drive a car because you still believe you have to hand-crank the engine to get it started.

Typical technical barriers include the following:

I need to learn a markup language

While it is true that early versions of wikis used a simple markup language known as wiki-text, and to complicate matters further, different wikis had their own versions, it is no longer true that you need to learn a markup language to use a wiki.

Nearly every wiki on the market today includes a rich text, word-processor-like, WYSIWYG editing tool. Anyone familiar with popular word processing applications can easily add formatted content to a wiki without ever seeing any markup. Most wikis present the rich text editing interface as the default.

Search doesn't work

The default search in many early wiki implementations fell short of expectations raised by the almost ubiquitous use of the Google search engine. Most current wikis, however, have either improved their native search engine or have extensions and plug-ins that vastly increase search capabilities.

Plugging the Google search engine into a wiki is also relatively straightforward. As highlighted in *Case Study 1*, WebWorks.com has integrated the Google search from its website so that searches not only return results from the site, but also from all its public knowledge bases, including the support database, customer project wikis, and documentation wikis.

In an article I wrote on wikis for the ars technica website (*Wikis in the workplace: a practical introduction*[1]), someone left a comment expressing the opinion that "it's less about search and more about organizing information." This is a very astute observation, as the most successful wikis don't just rely on a search functionality, but

---

[1] http://arstechnica.com/business/news/2009/11/welcome-to-the-wiki-party.ars/

also use Web 2.0 technology like tags and user-defined categories to organize information in a way that makes sense to the user community.

Turning on and encouraging such features will result in a wiki where navigation becomes a product of the users' actual requirements and behavior, rather than the result of a set of guesses by a data designer who's trying to predict which search terms and keywords will be popular.

It's a black hole

Many perceive that while it may be easy to get information into a wiki, it can be difficult to find and extract information. Others contend that a wiki can just degenerate into another file storage area, or download center. Both are symptoms of lack of organization and a failure to define what the role and purpose of the wiki should be.

Just putting a wiki in place is not a solution, because without some sort of direction it can quickly become a dumping ground, and without any oversight information can be lost. But the same could be said of any data storage system. These problems are not specific to wiki technology.

It isn't like (name your favorite application here)

No, wikis aren't like Microsoft Word, or Sharepoint, or any application you may already be familiar with, because they are designed for different purposes. One of the great strengths of a wiki is that it has many uses, and as such is often compared to existing applications that have been specifically designed to match one or more of those uses. But the essential thing to remember about wikis is that all wikis are based on the idea of an open, readily accessible platform – a web page that allows for collaboration and communication.

It's a security nightmare

The idea of an open, collaborative platform is seen by many as both a threat and a security nightmare. Yet, as I stated above, just because everyone can edit, doesn't mean that everyone will edit, or that everyone should be allowed to edit. Most wikis have excellent built-in security controls that allow you to restrict access to certain sections, categories, or even individual pages based on personal logins and user group settings. You can easily specify what you want people to see, what you want them to comment on, and what you want them to edit.

A general theme that runs through each of these discussion points is to make sure expectations are set before you implement and start using a wiki. And, remember that a wiki is all about collaboration and communication. Focus on that and not perceived barriers in the tool or the technology.

Appendix C

Anyone Can Edit: Myth vs. Reality

In all the conversations I have had about wiki technology and wiki implementation, the one item that constantly tops the lists of questions – or is raised as a first concern – is fear around the central concept of a wiki that anyone can edit.

Yes, wikis are designed to be open, and they are designed to encourage participation and collaboration. A wiki is designed to leverage the combined knowledge and experience of a community. But, as I hope we have shown in the preceding chapters, this doesn't inherently mean a lack of control, an invitation to vandalism, or a devaluing of the content. In fact the opposite is true; a well managed wiki means more control and higher quality information.

However, because the "anyone can edit" concept continues to raise questions, I decided to revisit it here and pull together some of the ideas discussed earlier as quick reference for anyone dealing with this particular issue.

Control

Just because a wiki has the capability to let anyone edit, it doesn't mean that anyone should edit. All wikis (including the most open and public ones) have some degree of control as to who can edit. Requiring users to log in allows you as the wiki owner to decide what you want people be allowed to do. That could be just read or comment on the text, but not make edits. Or, it might be the ability to overwrite and change existing content. Either way, that's a decision you can make.

Wikis have very granular controls that allow you to apply different permissions down to the individual page. For instance, on a company wiki an individual might have permission to edit pages that fit into his or her area of expertise, but permission only to comment on pages belonging to associated procedures, and only permission to read pages like HR policies. Some pages may be totally blocked from everyone except executive management.

If you follow the advice of this book and roll your wiki implementation out in a staged manner, you can start off by only giving access to a select few people, work out the structure and navigation issues, seed it with content, and then gradually open it up to more and more people. Again, the way you roll out access control is entirely up to you, but bear in mind that to really add value a wiki needs to be a reflection of the community it is intended to serve, and at some point all the members of that community will need some sort of access.

It is also worth remembering that on average the number of active contributors (i.e., those who will want to make edits on a regular basis) will be a subset of those who access the wiki. Depending on the size and function of the wiki, participation levels will most likely be between 1% and 30%

Vandalism

Media reports of vandalism on major public wiki sites are way out of proportion to the amount of overall activity on the sites. Yes, it does happen, but it is very rare. If you do have a vandalism problem, then you have a human relations, employee management issue rather than a technology one. If you make sure all wiki users have a login, then you can find the culprit quickly and take the appropriate action, which could range from simply suspending access for that account to disciplinary action for an errant employee. If someone does change a wiki page in a way that is deemed inappropriate, that page can be quickly and easily rolled back to the previous version.

Given the collaborative nature of a wiki, you may find heated discussions occurring in the wiki that would have previously been confined to private email or a face-to-face meeting. Your wiki administrators will have to set up ground rules and procedures to deal with things such as dueling edits or aggressive comment threads. However, experience has shown that most wiki communities are self-policing, and you should rarely need to put those policies into action.

Devalued Content

The myth of wiki inaccuracy has been addressed in several places in the preceding chapters, but it is worth reiterating that research and experience has repeatedly shown that wikis are at least as, and in many cases more, accurate in content than their traditional print counterparts.

The most successful wikis are those set up and used by teams and communities with shared interests and goals. As such they are read and monitored by subject matter experts and stake holders alike. Mistakes are quickly spotted and corrected, often in seconds. They also provide a place for the collective wisdom of the group to be captured and used by a much wider audience, often breaking down functional barriers, eliminating duplication of effort, and increasing understanding.

The true power of a wiki is not that anyone can edit, the true power of the wiki is that it promotes and enables collaboration.

Appendix D

Notes on Popular Wikis

This section provides brief overviews and notes on some of the more popular wiki platforms. Wikis included in this list are either mentioned in the main body of the book or were frequently mentioned by various users as I was researching information on wikis and wiki usage. It is not a comprehensive list of all available wiki platforms. To see a full list, visit Wiki Matrix http://www.wikimatrix.org.

Confluence

http://www.atlassian.com/software/confluence/
http://www.wikimatrix.org/show/Confluence

The Confluence wiki, from Atlassian software, is arguably the most widely deployed wiki platform in the enterprise market space. Confluence is designed specifically for enterprise use with unlimited wiki spaces, plus other features such as user networking tools, granular security, LDAP integration, and integrated search. Confluence ships with several functional level templates that enable quick setup and ease of use. It is also supported by an extensive library of third party plug-ins and integration with software development and publishing tools, which extend its capabilities. Confluence is available in either hosted or locally installed versions.

Intended Audience:	Technical teams in small, medium and enterprise-scale organizations.
License:	Proprietary, commercial software.

DokuWiki

http://www.dokuwiki.org/dokuwiki
http://www.wikimatrix.org/show/DokuWiki

DokuWiki is a simple to use Wiki, mainly aimed at creating documentation. It has a simple wiki-text syntax and does not require any supporting database. It is not designed for large knowledge management projects. There is a library of plug-ins available (Over 650 at the time of writing), which are created by the user community and aimed at extending the wiki's functionality.

Intended Audience: Developer teams, workgroups, small to medium companies.
License: Open Source (GPL version 2).

MediaWiki

http://www.mediawiki.org/wiki/MediaWiki
http://www.wikimatrix.org/show/MediaWiki

MediaWiki is perhaps the best known wiki platform, as it is the software used for Wikipedia (http://www.wikipedia.org) and the other Wikimedia Foundation websites. It is designed specifically for high traffic websites using multiple servers. It can be used for smaller applications, but the installation process can be complicated compared to other wikis. MediaWiki is open source software that can be freely downloaded. It is also available as a hosted service through http://www.wikia.com

Intended Audience: Education, Large High-Traffic Knowledge Bases.
License: Open Source (GPL version 2).

MindTouch

http://www.mindtouch.com/
http://www.wikimatrix.org/show/MindTouch

Originally derived from MediaWiki with a base of XHTML instead of wikitext and enhanced editing and search capabilities, the latest versions of the MindTouch platform allow users to integrate web services and external applications to extend the wiki's capabilities and enable data mashups. The platform is based on a open source project originally named DekiWiki that is supported by a large and active developer community. It has also been extended to provide the core for a range of products that make up an enterprise level collaboration platform.

Intended Audience:	Enterprise collaboration platform.
License:	Open Source (GPL version 2 and LGPL version 2.1).

MoinMoin

http://moinmo.in/
http://www.wikimatrix.org/show/MoinMoin

MoinMoin is an advanced, easy to use, fast and modular Wiki engine written in Python. Its storage model is based on flat files and folders, rather than a database. MoinMoin supports plug-ins and can also be extended through the use of macros. Users can choose between using the built-in search functions or a third party search engine. MoinMoin is popular in the software development community.

Intended Audience:	Small to medium size workgroups and businesses.
License:	Open Source (GPL version 2).

MyWiki

http://www.mywikiapp.com/
Not listed on the WikiMatri.

MyWiki is a personal wiki application designed for iPhone users to provide a central place to store information, links and notes, using a wiki format.

Intended Audience:	Individuals.
License:	Commercial ($2.99 in iPhone app store).

PBworks

http://pbworks.com
http://www.wikimatrix.org/show/PBwiki

PBworks has traditionally been focused on being simpler and easier to use than most other wiki platforms. It offers two levels of access, a free version that has most of the functionality needed by individuals or small workgroups, and a paid version that offers more functionality. PBworks also supplies paying customers with templates and wikis pre-configured for certain industry applications, such as its Legal and Campus editions. (This book was written, edited, reviewed, and published using PBworks.)

Intended Audience:	Businesses.
License:	Proprietary, available as free or premium hosted service.

ProjectForum

http://www.projectforum.com/pf/
http://www.wikimatrix.org/show/ProjectForum

ProjectForum is designed to enable collaboration between small to medium sized project teams. It is easy to install and use with no separate web server, database, or version control system. ProjectForum offers both downloadable and hosted versions.

Intended Audience:	Small to medium-sized workgroups, in a wide variety of settings (small-large business, non-profit, research, education, etc.).
License:	Proprietary, available as free personal version, or various paid commercial versions.

TiddlyWiki

http://www.tiddlywiki.com/
http://www.wikimatrix.org/show/TiddlyWiki

TiddlyWiki is a single-page application designed to be used as a personal notebook. TiddlyWiki can be used for personal, self-contained hypertext documents that can be posted to any web-server, sent by email or kept on a USB thumb drive. TiddlyWiki is highly customizable and has an active community of developers and users.

Intended Audience:	Individuals, small groups.
License:	Open Source (BSD).

TikiWIki

http://tiki.org/
http://www.wikimatrix.org/show/Tiki-Wiki

TikiWiki is a free and open source wiki-based, content management system. Also know simply as "Tiki," this wiki contains a large number of collaboration features including blogs, calendars, forums, faqs, and other groupware capabilities. The XML Press reader's wiki, http://readers.xmlpress.net, uses TikiWiki.

Intended Audience:	Groups needing a wide variety of built-in features.
License:	Open Source (Lesser GPL).

Trac

http://trac.edgewall.org/
http://www.wikimatrix.org/show/TracWiki

Trac is an enhanced wiki and issue tracking system for software development projects. Trac allows wiki markup in issue descriptions and commit messages, creating links and seamless references between bugs, tasks, change sets, files, and wiki pages. A timeline shows all project events in order, making getting an overview of the project and tracking progress very easy.

Intended Audience:	Software developers.
License:	Open Source (modified BSD).

Resources

Books

[1] Barabási, Albert-László. *Linked: How Everything is Connected to Everything Else and What it Means*. Plume, 2003, ISBN: 978-0452284395.

[2] Brown, M. Katherine, Brenda Huettner, and Char James-Tanny. *Managing Virtual Teams: Getting the most from Wikis, Blogs and Other Collaborative Tools*. Jones & Bartlett, 2007, ISBN: 978-1598220285.

[3] Leuf, Bo and Ward Cunningham. *The Wiki Way: Quick Collaboration on the Web*. Addison-Wesley, 2001, ISBN: 978-0201714999.

[4] Gentle, Anne. *Conversation and Community: The Social Web for Documentation*. XML Press, 2009, ISBN: 978-0-9822191-1-9.

[5] Mader, Stewart. *Wikipatterns*. Wiley, 2007, ISBN: 978-0-470-22362-8.

[6] Merchant, Nilofer. *The New How: Creating Business Solutions through Collaborative Strategy*. O'Reilly, 2010, ISBN: 978-0-596-15625-1.

[7] Porter, Alan. *Before They Were Beatles*. Xlibris, 2003, ISBN: 978-1413430561.

[8] Sun Microsystems. *Writing in the Open: Using Wikis to Create Documentation*. Vervante, 2009, ISBN: 978-0595352692.

[9] Tapscott, Don and Anthony D. Williams. *Wikinomics: How Mass Collaboration Changes Everything*. Portfolio, 2006, ISBN: 978-1591841388.

Web Sites

[10] Creative Commons Licenses: http://creativecommons.org

[11] WikiMatrix.org Comparison Web Site: http://www.wikimatrix.org

[12] Wikipatterns Web Site: http://wikipatterns.com

Other Sources

[13] "Using a Wiki to Implement a Quality Management System." Castano, Francisco, Gerardo Mendez, Julio Ayala, and Linda Day. Quality Digest Daily. October, 2009. http://creativecommons.org

Acknowledgments

While the title of this book may be focused on the word WIKI as a technology, in fact this is a book about collaboration, and any book, even one with a single author's name on the cover, is in fact an exercise in collaboration. Projects like this can never be done alone, and I have been very lucky to have such a great team of collaborators with me, helping pull my ideas together and make this book a reality.

First off I'd like to thank XML Press Publisher Richard Hamilton for agreeing to help turn my various ramblings and ideas about wiki implementation into a book. Also a big vote of thanks to *The Content Wrangler* himself, Scott Abel, for introducing me to Richard in the first place and for providing the foreword to the book. My fellow XML Press authors, Anne Gentle, Zarella Rendon and Brenda Huettner were a great team of cheer leaders. Thanks also to Scott, Anne, and Brenda for being part of the review team, along with Mike Aragona, Jay Willson, and Sarah Maddox. All of them provided great notes, helped me overcome certain assumptions and preconceived ideas, and helped make the book a much better read.

I'd also like to thank wiki evangelist, Stewart Mader, for some excellent conference bar conversations and for sharing his infectious enthusiasm for the wiki's potential. The team at WebWorks.com in Austin, TX, Tony McDow, Ben Allums, and Jesse Wiles, deserve a note of thanks for introducing me to the practicalities of using, managing, and publishing with wikis in a business environment. Thanks are also due to the folks at Atlassian software, makers of the Confluence Wiki, for being such great hosts when I visited their San Francisco offices to talk wikis.

I am indebted to Noelle Thurlow and Francisco "Pancho" Castano for sharing a panel at the WikiSym 2009 conference with me and for giving me permission to use their wiki stories as case studies. A vote of thanks also goes to Gina Fevrier for permission to use her STC presentation as the basis for a case study.

A special mention to my two artistic collaborators on this project, Patrick Davison for the excellent cover design, and Doug Potter for the fun cartoons. It was a pleasure working with both of you.

But, as always, the biggest vote of thanks goes to my family, my wonderful wife, Gill, and my two daughters, Meggan and Erin, for their support and for putting up with the many evenings of me disappearing into my home office to hit the keyboard. They are the best collaborative team that anyone could ever wish for.

Alan J. Porter
September, 2010
Austin, Texas

Index

Coming Soon from XML Press

The Content Pool, by Alan J. Porter

All companies, no matter what industry they are in or what product or service they create, do four basic things. Offer something for sale, sell it, collect the money for it, and create content about it.

Product development, Marketing, Sales, and Finance are all recognized as essential to the organization and are often reflected by VP or CXO level responsibility, yet a company's content, which contains all of its intellectual property, is often overlooked.

Whether you know it or not, your company is a publisher.

Alan J. Porter's forthcoming book, *The Content Pool: How to Identify, Organize, Manage, and Leverage Your Company's Largest Hidden Asset*, makes the case for placing content creation, management, and distribution on a par with other core strategic business activities.

The book will explore:

- Why every company is a publisher
- What content do you produce now, and how do you use it?
- Identifying the audience, today and in the future
- Is the language you use costing you money or even making you legally liable?
- Content development silos – gain through collaboration
- How consistency saves you money
- Where are your pain points?
- Styles and Standards
- Rewrite and reuse
- It's about answers, not the documentation
- Your customers will add value to your content
- Technology comes last
- Your content can be a revenue source
- Good content wins customers

- ► Helpful content reduces support costs
- ► Develop a Content Strategy

The book will conclude with – The Case for having a CCO (Chief Content Officer).

The Content Pool is scheduled for publication in 2011.

About the Author

Alan Porter has 20 plus years experience in corporate communications, marketing, and content development in both the UK and the USA. Alan is a catalyst for change with a strong track record in developing new ideas, embracing emerging technologies, and introducing operational improvements. He has been involved in the development and adoption of various industry standards, and is a regular speaker at industry conferences, who is happy to talk communications to anyone who will listen.

He is also a published author with several books, comics and numerous magazine articles to his name.

You can find full details of Alan J. Porter's books as well as signing and speaking engagements at his website: http://alanjporter.com.

You can follow him on Twitter at @alanjporter (for general writing and slice of life topics), or @4jsgroup (for technical and corporate communications topics).

THE CONTENT POOL, his blog on various thoughts and opinions on corporate communications and digital publishing can be found at http://thecontentpool.com

The Content Pool is also the title of his next book from XML Press, due in 2011.